ideas

# ideas

open spaces
espacios abiertos
espaces ouverts
offene bereiche

AUTHORS
Fernando de Haro & Omar Fuentes

EDITORIAL DESIGN & PRODUCTION

EDITORES    PUBLISHERS

PROJECT MANAGERS
Carlos Herver Díaz
Ana Teresa Vázquez de la Mora
Laura Mijares Castellá

COORDINATION
Emily Keime López
Verónica Velasco Joos
Dulce María Rodríguez Flores

PREPRESS COORDINATION
José Luis de la Rosa Meléndez

COPYWRITER
Víctor Hugo Martínez

ENGLISH TRANSLATION
Michel Moric Altaras

FRENCH TRANSLATION
Angloamericano de Cuernavaca - Carmen Chalamanch . Marta Pou

GERMAN TRANSLATION
Angloamericano de Cuernavaca - Sabine Klein

Ideas
open spaces · espacios abiertos
espaces ouverts · offene bereiche

© 2012, Fernando de Haro & Omar Fuentes

AM Editores S.A. de C.V.
Paseo de Tamarindos 400 B, suite 102, Col. Bosques de las Lomas,
C.P. 05120, México, D.F., Tel. 52(55) 5258 0279
E-mail: ame@ameditores.com    www.ameditores.com

ISBN: 978-607-437-219-9

Printed in China.

# introduction    introducción

Open spaces are the alternate face of architecture; that of the vacuum, of nothingness, or of the mere absence of volume. While everything that is considered a living space is inevitably linked to something that is constructed or adapted by men, the absence of volume and construction in architecture is a great revelation when talking about comfort. A perfect balance to satisfy the needs of everyday life.

Los espacios abiertos configuran el rostro alterno de la arquitectura, el del vacío, la ausencia o la nada. Si bien todo lo que se considera un espacio habitable se vincula irremediablemente al espacio construido o adaptado por el hombre, el vacío en la arquitectura, la ausencia de construcción en volumen es otra de las grandes revelaciones del confort. Un equilibrio perfecto para satisfacer la vida diaria.

# introduction    einleitung

Les espaces ouverts forment l'autre visage de l'architecture, celui du vide, l'absence, le néant. Si tout ce qui est considéré comme un espace habitable est relié inévitablement à l'espace construit et adapté par l'homme, le vide en architecture, l'absence de construction en volume, est une autre des grandes révélations du confort. Un équilibre parfait pour satisfaire la vie quotidienne.

Offene Räume sind die andere Seite der Architektur, die der Leere, des Fehlens oder des Nichts. Wenn auch alles, was als ein bewohnbarer Bereich betrachtet wird, unwillkürlich mit etwas Gebautem oder von einem Menschen bewohnbar gemachten, in Verbindung gebracht wird, ist das Fehlen einer Bebauung eine andere der grossen Offenbarungen des Komforts. Ein perfekter Ausgleich für ein befriedigendes tägliches Leben.

Spaces that are not interfered with on a large scale are primarily meeting points and social interaction centers by excellence. Some have the quality of being transient, others are made to be contemplated, and some provide us with an experience that is out of the ordinary. Due to all these qualities, these spaces should not be treated as unimportant or supporting players in the realm of architecture. Indeed, in many cases they are the window into the soul of a place, where social interaction is vibrant and family values are personified. They are sometimes the most intimate spaces of all, where comfort reaches a level of dream: outdoor living areas.

No rule has ever been written regarding the design of these areas, but it is widely known that they function as an extension of nature. Whereby they are visualized as places full of light, they allow one to rest, relax, or simply contemplate the passing of time while staring at the horizon. Hence the importance of examining different aspects during their conception, such as the

Los espacios no intervenidos a gran escala, aquellos que quedan a la intemperie son lugares de encuentro e interacción social por excelencia, algunos con la cualidad de ser transitorios, otros dispuestos para ser contemplados y unos más para brindarnos una experiencia fuera de lo cotidiano. Por todo lo anterior, no son espacios secundarios que deban quedar relegados ni carecer de importancia, son en muchos casos el rostro de un hogar a través de la fachada; el punto de mayor interacción social o vínculo familiar personificado en una alberca o canal de nado y, finalmente también ese espacio favorito de privilegio, quizá más íntimo donde la comodidad alcanza un nivel de ensueño: la terraza.

Ninguna regla se ha escrito en cuanto al diseño de estas áreas pero debe saberse que funcionan como extensiones de la naturaleza que al ser pensados como lugares llenos de luz permiten el descanso, la relajación o sencillamente la contemplación del paso del tiempo en el horizonte. De ahí la importancia que

Les espaces non intervenus à grande échelle, ceux qui sont laissés sans abri, sont les endroits de rencontre et interaction sociales par excellence, certains ayant la qualité d'être transitoires, d'autres prêts à être contemplés et d'autres encore à nous donner une expérience hors du quotidien. C'est pour cela que ce ne sont pas des espaces secondaires qui doivent être laissés de côté ou qui sont sans importance, car ce sont souvent le visage d'une maison à travers la façade ; le point de plus grande interaction sociale ou de liens de famille personnifié par une piscine ou canal de nage, et finalement, aussi cet espace favori de privilège, peut-être le plus intime où le confort atteint un niveau de rêve : la terrasse.

Il n'y a aucune règle écrite quant au design de ces espaces, mais on doit savoir qu'ils fonctionnent comme des extensions de la nature, qui, étant conçus comme des espaces pleins de lumière, permettent le repos, la détente, ou tout simplement la contemplation du temps qui passe à l'horizon. De

Grossflächige, unberührte Bereiche unter freiem Himmel sind ideale Orte für Begegnunten oder ein geselliges Zusammensein, einige sind Durchgangszonen, andere laden zum Betrachten ein und wieder andere bieten uns ein aussergewöhnliches Erlebnis. Daher sind sie keine zweitrangigen Bereiche, die weder vernachlässigt werden sollten, noch an Wichtigkeit einbussen dürfen; in vielen Fällen sind sie das Gesicht eines Heimes hinter der Fassade; der Ort mit der grössten sozialen Interaktion oder persönlichen familiären Beziehungen in einem Schwimmbecken oder Schwimmkanal und nicht zuletzt auch der Lieblingsplatz per se, vielleicht der intimste, in dem die Annehmlichkeiten ein traumhaftes Niveau erreichen: die Terrasse.

Es gibt in diesem Bereich keine geschriebenen Regeln, aber man sollte wissen, dass sie wie eine Erweiterung de Natur funktionieren, die als mit Licht gefüllte Orte Erholung, Entspannung oder einfach nur das Betrachten des Verlaufes der Zeit am Horizont, erlauben.

relationship with the landscape surrounding them, the selection and design of the gardening tools and concepts, the presence or lack of decorative elements, a thorough lighting design, the weather, the kind and variety of materials to be used, and even the optimum size of the whole space, all to avoid unnecessary expenses and headaches.

Architecture and the design of outdoor areas, like art in general, is responsible for creating the perfect setting for an everyday experience, and regulating the interactions between the environment, the living space, nature, and the user. For this to occur, there must be unity; a relationship with the landscape, with the geometry of the area, as well as with the five senses, all to produce an emotional reaction that will transform the perception of the ordinary into a unique, peculiar, and above all pleasurable experience.

This volume represents a valuable compendium of solutions for different types of environments such as the city, the countryside, and the beach. It is clear that each of these environments is unique, so we demonstrate and teach the most effective methods to highlight elements that, when in harmony, favor its design. The delight of seeing architecture is present in these pages, and this is simply an invitation to enjoy it.

tiene examinar diferentes aspectos en su concepción tales como la relación que éstos mantienen con el paisaje que los rodea, la selección y diseño de la jardinería, la presencia o privación de elementos decorativos, el diseño integral de iluminación, el clima del sitio, la paleta de materiales a emplear y hasta el tamaño idóneo para no caer en gastos e inclusive derroches innecesarios.

La arquitectura y el diseño de espacios abiertos tal como el arte en general tiene el papel de construir el marco perfecto para la experiencia cotidiana, regular las interacciones entre el medio, el espacio o la naturaleza y el usuario. Para que esto se produzca debe existir una unidad; un vínculo con el paisaje, con la geometría así como con los cinco sentidos para producir un estímulo emocional que transforme a percepción de lo común en una experiencia peculiar, novedosa y sobre todo acogedora.

Este volumen representa un valioso compendio de soluciones para distintos tipos de ambientes como son la ciudad, el campo o la playa. Es evidente que cada uno posee un código peculiar por lo cual en estas páginas se hace notar los valores de cada uno de ellos, así como la manera más eficaz de resaltar elementos que en armonía favorecen su diseño. El deleite de ver arquitectura se hace presente en estas páginas, esta sólo es la invitación para disfrutarla.

là l'importance d'examiner les différents aspects de leur conception, tels que leur relation avec le paysage qui les entoure, le choix et le design du jardinage, la présence ou absence d'éléments de décoration, le design intégral de l'éclairage, le climat local, la palette de matériaux à employer, jusqu'à la taille idéale pour ne pas sombrer dans des coûts, ou même des gaspillages inutiles.

L'architecture et le design des espaces ouverts, ainsi que l'art en général, doit construire le cadre parfait pour l'expérience quotidienne, régler les échanges entre le milieu, l'espace ou la nature, et l'usager. Pour ceci, il doit y avoir une unité, un lien avec le paysage, avec la géométrie, ainsi qu'avec les cinq sens, pour produire un stimulus émotionnel qui transforme la perception du commun en une expérience distinctive, nouvelle, et, surtout, accueillante.

Ce volume représente un recueil précieux de solutions pour les différents types d'ambiances, telles que la ville, la campagne ou la plage. Il est évident que chacune d'elles possède un code particulier, c'est pourquoi ces pages soulignent les valeurs de chacune d'elles, ainsi que la manière la plus efficace de rehausser les éléments dont l'harmonie favorise le design. Le plaisir de voir l'architecture apparaît dans ces pages, et ce n'est qu'une invitation à l'apprécier.

Daher ist es wichtig die verschiedenen Aspekte ihrer Planung zu bedenken, wie die Beziehung, die sie mit der sie umgebenden Landschaft haben, die Auswahl und das Design ihrer Bepflanzung, die Präsenz oder das Fehlen von dekorativen Elementen, das Design ihrer Beleuchtung, das Klima des Ortes, die Wahl der benutzten Materialien und sogar die ideale Grösse um nicht in unnötige Ausgaben und sogar Verschwendung zu verfallen.

Die Architektur und das Design offener Bereiche, wie Kunst im allgemeinen, hat die Aufgabe einen perfekten Rahmen für ein alltägliches Erlebnis zu schaffen, die Beziehung zwischen der Umgebung, dem Bereich oder der Natur und dem Benutzer zu steuern. Um das zu erreichen sollte eine Einheit existieren; eine Verbindung mit der Landschaft, mit der Geometrie sowie den fünf Sinnen, um einen emotionalen Reiz zu schaffen, der die Wahrnehmung des Alltäglichen in ein besonderes Erlebnis, neu und vor allem angenehm, verwandelt.

Dieses Buch präsentiert eine wertvolle Sammlung von Lösungen für verschiedene Ambiente wie es die Stadt, das Land oder der Strand sind. Es ist offensichtlich, dass jedes einzelne einem besonderen Gesetz folgt, weswegen auf diesen Seiten der Wert jedes einzelnen bemerkt wird, sowie die beste Art Elemente herauszustellen, die harmonisch ihrem Design zugute kommen. Der Genuss Architektur zu sehen, wird auf diesen Seiten deutlich, es ist eine Einladung sie zu geniessen.

countryside · campo
campagne · land

A sober composition in the façade design can enhance the relationship between the interior and the exterior components of an architectural project. The large windows and the modest details in the aluminum works, in conjunction with the furniture, allow one to appreciate the immense garden, which is the area of greatest relevance.

Una composición sobria en el diseño de la fachada puede exaltar la relación entre interior y exterior de un proyecto arquitectónico. Los amplios ventanales así como los modestos detalles en la cancelería en conjunto con el mobiliario permiten apreciar el inmenso jardín, el espacio de mayor relevancia.

Une composition sobre du design de la façade peut exalter la relation entre l'intérieur et l'extérieur d'un projet architectural. Les amples fenêtres ainsi que les détails modestes des châssis unis au mobilier permettent d'apprécier l'immense jardin, l'espace le plus important.

Eine schmucklose Komposition des Fassadendesigns kann die Beziehung zwischen den Innen- und Aussenbereichen eines baulichen Projektes herausstellen. Die grossen Wandfenster, sowie die schlichten Details der Türen und Fenster, zusammen mit den Möbeln, erlauben es den Garten zu würdigen, den Bereich mit der grössten Bedeutung.

THE PRESENCE OF A LARGE DECK covered with clay tiles and wooden beams evokes the image of the traditional cottage house. However, when you add a variety of materials to the furniture, the coatings and colors give it a great contemporary touch. The fireplace and its design can be crucial depending on the climate of the space.

LA PRESENCIA DE UNA GRAN CUBIERTA revestida de tejas de barro y las vigas de madera evocan la tradicional casa de campo, sin embargo incluir una selecta diversidad de materiales en el mobiliario, los recubrimientos y los acentos de color le dan un gran toque contemporáneo. La chimenea y su diseño puede ser un elemento fundamental dependiendo el clima que el lugar posea.

LA PRÉSENCE D'UNE GRANDE TOITURE revêtue de tuiles en terre glaise et les poutres en bois évoquent la maison de campagne traditionnelle, mais en incluant une diversité bien choisie de matériaux pour le mobilier, les revêtements et les accents de couleur, on obtient un air très contemporain. La cheminée et son design peuvent constituer un élément fondamental selon le climat local.

DIE PRÄSENZ EINES GROSSEN DACHES mit Tonziegeln gedeckt und die Holzbalken, erwecken den Eindruck eines traditionellen Landhauses, die Verwendung verschiedener, ausgesuchter Materialien bei den Möbeln, den Verkleidungen und den Farbakzenten, gibt ihm eine starke zeitgenössische Note. Der Kamin und sein Design können, abhängend von dem Klima in dem sich das Haus befindet, ein fundamentales Element sein.

To gaze at a façade design can be a very pleasant daily experience. Thus, transition zones can be embellished with a mirror of water and the presence of stone elements or medium-sized sculptures. Lighting plays a fundamental role in highlighting the relationship between solid and empty spaces of the design.

Disfrutar del diseño de la fachada puede ser una experiencia diaria muy grata, para ello se recurre a zonas de transición embellecidas con un espejo de agua y la presencia de elementos pétreos o esculturas de formato medio. La iluminación juega un papel fundamental para resaltar la relación de vanos y macizos del diseño formal del proyecto.

Apprécier le design de la façade peut être une expérience quotidienne très agréable, et pour cela on utilise les zones de transition embellies par un miroir d'eau et la présence d'éléments de pierre ou de sculptures de format moyen. L'éclairage joue un rôle fondamental pour rehausser la relation des embrasures et des parties massives du design formel du projet.

Sich am Design der Fassade zu erfreuen kann ein sehr angenehmes tägliches Erlebnis sein, dazu dienen Übergangsbereiche, die mit einem Wasserspiegel und der Präsenz von Elementen aus Stein oder Skulpturen mittlerer Grösse verschönert werden. Die Beleuchtung spielt eine fundamentale Rolle, um die Beziehung zwischen leeren und massiven Flächen des formellen Designs des Projektes zu unterstreichen.

swimming pools
piscinas
piscines
schwimmbecken

THE LOCATION of a pool is in itself one of the main elements to be decided upon, depending on its frequency of use, weather, or the visual settings that it can provide of the surrounding landscape. The field offers great sunsets and in many cases, the vegetation is as attractive as the pool itself. The relationship between the existing, natural space and the built space is what makes the experience a much more pleasant one.

LA UBICACIÓN MISMA de una piscina es uno de los elementos principales a definir dependiendo de su frecuencia de uso, el clima o los encuadres visuales que ésta pueda darnos con respecto al paisaje circundante. El campo ofrece grandes atardeceres y en muchos de los casos la vegetación es tan atractiva como el diseño mismo. Procurar la relación entre lo existente del sitio y lo intervenido hará que la experiencia sea mucho más placentera.

L'EMPLACEMENT MÊME de la piscine est un des éléments principaux à définir, selon la fréquence avec laquelle on l'utilise, le climat ou les cadres visuels qu'elle peut nous donner en relation avec le paysage qui l'entoure. La campagne offre de beaux couchers de soleil et souvent la végétation est aussi attrayante que le design lui-même. Si on obtient la relation entre ce qui existe localement et ce qui est créé, on aura une expérience beaucoup plus agréable.

DIE LAGE eines Schwimmbeckens an sich ist eins der Hauptelemente, das definiert werden muss, abhängig von der Häufigkeit seiner Nutzung, dem Klima und, den Rahmen den es uns für die umgebende Landschaft geben kann. Das Land bietet spektakuläre Sonnenuntergänge und in vielen Fällen ist der Pflanzenwuchs genauso attraktiv wie das Design selbst. Eine Verbindung zwischen dem Bestehenden und dem Geschaffenen zu herzustellen, macht das Erlebnis sehr viel reizvoller.

THE MONOCHROMATIC DESIGN of the cottage can merge elegantly with a coating of light shades on the pool. The reflexes accentuate the sophisticated conception of space without reducing the neatness of the space as a whole.

EL DISEÑO MONOCROMÁTICO de la casa de campo puede fusionarse de manera elegante con un recubrimiento en tonos claros en la alberca. Los reflejos acentuarán la sofisticada concepción del espacio sin reducir la pulcritud del conjunto.

LE DESIGN MONOCHROME de la maison de campagne peut se fusionner de manière élégante avec un revêtement en tons clairs dans la piscine. Les reflets accentueront la conception sophistiquée de l'espace sans diminuer la pureté de l'ensemble.

DAS EINFARBIGE DESIGN des Landhauses kann auf elegante Weise mit den Verkleidungen in hellen Tönen des Schwimmbeckens verschmelzen. Die Spiegelungen betonen das raffinierte Konzept des Bereiches, ohne die Reinheit des Ganzen zu beeinträchtigen.

The dimensions of these spaces are linked to its social function: a smaller pool can be located in an interior for restricted use by the inhabitants, and a larger one will generally be located outside to facilitate the interaction between a larger group of people.

Las dimensiones de estos espacios se vinculan a su función social: una piscina más pequeña puede ubicarse en un interior para uso restringido de los habitantes, una más grande generalmente será ubicada en el exterior para favorecer la interacción de un grupo mayor de personas.

Les dimensions de ces espaces sont liées à leur fonction sociale : une piscine plus petite peut être située à l'intérieur pour l'usage exclusif des habitants, tandis qu'une piscine plus grande sera située généralement à l'extérieur pour favoriser l'interaction d'un groupe plus important de personnes.

Die Grösse dieser Bereiche sind an ihre soziale Funktion geknüpft: ein kleineres Schwimmbecken kann man im Innenbereich anlegen, für denalleinigen Nutzen der Bewohner, ein grösseres wird gemeinhin im Aussenbereich angelegt, um die Nutzung durch eine grössere Gruppe zu erleichtern.

The precautions with construction details go hand in hand with the choice of suitable materials that must be used when you built structures that will be used when walking on these humid zones, so security is as important as comfort and the presence of visual details.

El cuidado de los detalles constructivos va de la mano de la selección de materiales adecuados para transitar estas zonas húmedas, la seguridad es tan prioritaria como la comodidad y la presencia de detalles o remates visuales en estos espacios.

Le soin prêté aux détails de construction va de pair avec le choix des matériaux appropriés pour se déplacer dans ces zones humides, la sécurité étant aussi prioritaire que le confort et la présence de détails ou de couronnements visuels dans ces espaces.

Zur Sorgfalt bei den baulichen Details gehört auch die Auswahl angemessener Materialien für die begehbaren Flächen in Nasszonen, die Sicherheit ist genauso wichtig wie der Komfort und die Präsenz von Details oder optischen Abschlüssen in diesen Bereichen.

Be aware that the correspondence between geometric shapes, tonalities, and materials helps you to have a harmonious perception of the space, by conveying a message of serenity.

Vigilar la correspondencia entre formas geométricas, tonalidades y materiales beneficia la percepción armónica del espacio al transmitir un mensaje de serenidad y armonía.

Soigner la correspondance des formes géométriques, les tonalités et les matériaux favorise la perception harmonieuse de l'espace en transmettant un message de sérénité et harmonie.

Das Verhältnis zwischen geometrischen Formen, Farbtönen und Materialen kommt dem harmonischen Eindruck des Bereiches zugute, indem es eine Botschaft von Ruhe und Harmonie vermittelt.

The temperature of the light can be operated within contrasting scenes. For example, use warm light to emphasize the architectural elements, and make use of cold light in the pool or in the jacuzzi. The tonalities that you will obtain from this will evoke a harmonious relationship between water and fire in the exterior area.

La temperatura de la luz puede manejarse dentro de escenas contrastantes; por ejemplo, emplear luz cálida para enfatizar los elementos arquitectónicos y, hacer uso de luz fría en la alberca o en el jacuzzi. Las tonalidades obtenidas evocarán gratamente la relación agua y fuego en el espacio exterior.

La température de la lumière peut être manipulée dans des scènes contrastantes ; par exemple, l'utilisation de la lumière chaude pour rehausser les éléments architecturels, et la lumière froide dans la piscine ou le jacuzzi. Les tonalités obtenues évoqueront agréablement la relation de l'eau et le feu dans l'espace extérieur.

Die Temperatur des Lichts kann man innerhalb kontrastierender Szenen handhaben; zum Beispiel warmes Licht, um die architektonischen Elemente zu betonen und kaltes Licht für das Schwimmbecken oder den Jacuzzi. Die erhaltenen Farbtöne lassen im Aussenbereich auf angenehme Weise an die Beziehung Wasser – Feuer denken.

terraces terrazas terrasses terrassen

THE DESIGN OF THE TERRACE must fulfill the mission of allowing us to rest in comfort for a long period of time. In these areas the provision of furniture should facilitate communication and eye contact between users as well as seek an intimate relationship with those areas worthy of contemplation. Elements such as pergolas and chimneys ensure that the space can be used during the day or during the night, and always provide a pleasant experience.

EL DISEÑO DE UNA TERRAZA debe cumplir a cabalidad la misión de reconfortarnos durante un largo periodo de tiempo. En estos espacios la disposición de los muebles debe favorecer la comunicación y el contacto visual entre los usuarios así como procurar una intima relación con aquellas zonas dignas de contemplación. Elementos como pérgolas o chimeneas propician que su utilidad durante el día o la noche sea siempre placentera.

LE DESIGN D'UNE TERRASSE doit achever totalement la mission de nous procurer du confort pendant une longue période de temps. Dans ces espaces, la disposition des meubles doit favoriser la communication et le contact visuel, ainsi qu'une relation intime avec les zones dignes d'être contemplées. Certains éléments tels les pergolas ou les cheminées favorisent son utilité aussi bien le jour que la nuit.

DAS DESIGN EINER TERRASSE muss auf jeden Fall die Mission erfüllen uns für einen langen Zeitraum einen Zufluchtsort zu gewähren. In diesen Bereichen sollte die Anordnung der Möbel die Kommunikation und den Augenkontakt zwischen den Benutzern erleichtern, sowie eine intime Beziehung zu den betrachtenswerten Bereichen sicherstellen. Elemente wie Pergolas oder Kamine lassen seine Nutzung während des Tages oder des Abends immer angenehm werden.

WHEN CHOOSING FURNITURE, one must always be aware of what kind of materials they are made from, and if they are resistant to their surroundings and the climate of the place in which will be used. Apart from their aesthetic qualities, these pieces must ultimately provide comfort.

EL MOBILIARIO A ESCOGER debe de contar con materiales resistentes a la intemperie de acuerdo al clima del lugar en el que serán empleados. Más allá de sus cualidades estéticas la importancia en su selección recae en la comodidad que nos otorgan.

LE MOBILIER CHOISI doit posséder des matériaux résistants adaptés au climat local. Au-delà de ses qualités esthétiques, l'importance du choix dépend du confort qu'il nous procure.

DIE MÖBEL SOLLTEN aus wetterfestem Material gearbeitet sein, abhängig von dem Klima in dem sich gebotene Bequemlichkeit, ein wichtiger Punkt bei ihrer Wahl.

Wood coatings harmonize with the beauty of the natural setting; the use of furniture or cushions in pastel hues accentuates the feeling of freshness and serenity in the space.

Los recubrimientos en madera permiten armonizar con la belleza del contexto natural; usar algunos muebles o cojines en tonos pastel acentúan la sensación de frescura y serenidad en el espacio.

Les revêtements en bois permettent l'harmonie avec la beauté du contexte naturel ; quelques meubles ou coussins en tons pastel accentuent la sensation de fraîcheur et de sérénité dans l'espace.

Verkleidungen aus Holz erlauben mit der natürlichen Umgeben in Harmonie zu stehen; einige Möbel oder Kissen in Pastelltönen zu verwendung, betont den frischen und ruhigen Eindruck des Bereiches.

When a terrace is immersed in a natural environment of great beauty, it is advisable to use a decorative element that through its simplicity reiterates the visual hierarchy of the landscape, an evocation to freedom and contemplation.

Cuando una terraza se encuentra inmersa en un entorno natural de gran belleza resulta confortable emplear algún elemento decorativo o mobiliario que con su sencillez nos reitere la jerarquía visual que posee el paisaje, una evocación a la libertad y la contemplación.

Quand une terrasse est immergée dans un entourage naturel de grande beauté, il est confortable d'utiliser un élément décoratif ou un mobilier dont la simplicité nous souligne la hiérarchie visuelle que possède le paysage, une évocation de la liberté et la contemplation.

Wenn eine Terrasse in eine natürliche Umgebung von grosser Schönheit eingebettet ist, ist es angebracht irgendein dekoratives Element oder Möbelstück zu verwenden, dass mit seiner Schlichtheit die optische Hierarchie der Landschaft wiederholt, die Freiheit beschwört und zur Betrachtung einlädt.

WHEN THERE IS A DOMINATING PRESENCE OF WOOD and we have selected various shades within our terrace, it is recommended that the structure of the pergola be designed with steel profiles and that these are painted in dark colors. The presence of those tones will merge beautifully with the vast amount of light that the wood will receive, and at the same time will add elegance to the main furniture pieces of the space.

CUANDO EXISTE UNA PRESENCIA DOMINANTE DE MADERA y se han seleccionado diversas tonalidades dentro de nuestra terraza es recomendable que la estructura de la pérgola sea diseñada con perfiles de acero y que éstos sean pintados en colores oscuros. La presencia de esos tonos se vinculará bien a la inmensa cantidad de luz que recibirá la madera, del mismo modo podrá relacionarse con los muebles protagónicos del espacio.

QUAND LA PRÉSENCE DU BOIS EST DOMINANTE et qu'on a sélectionné diverses tonalités dans notre terrasse, il est recommandable que la structure de la pergola soit faite de tiges d'acier peintes en couleurs foncées. La présence de ces tons aura une bonne relation avec l'immense quantité de lumière que recevra le bois, et pourra de la même façon dialoguer avec les meubles dominant l'espace.

WENN HOLZ DAS DOMINIERENDE MATERIAL ist und verschiedene Holztöne innerhalb der Terrasse gewählt wurden, ist es zu empfehlen, das Gerüst der Pergola aus Stahl zu entwerfen und es in dunklen Farben zu streichen. Diese Farböne verbinden sich gut mit der enormen Lichtmenge die das Holz empfängt, und gleichzeitig können sie einen Bezug auf die im Mittelpunkt stehenden Möbel herstellen.

The texture of stone coatings can be elegantly contrasted with the softness of white color and its attribute to generate an atmosphere full of freshness, spaciousness and quiet for resting.

La textura de los recubrimientos pétreos puede contrastarse elegantemente con la suavidad del color blanco y su cualidad de generar una atmósfera colmada de frescura, amplitud y sosiego para el descanso.

La texture des revêtements de pierre peut être mise en contraste élégant avec la douceur de la couleur blanche et sa capacité de créer une atmosphère pleine de fraîcheur, amplitude et tranquillité pour le repos.

Die Textur der Steinverkleidungen steht auf elegante Weise in Kontrast zu dem weichen Weiss und seiner Eigenschaft eine frische, weite und beschauliche Atmosphäre zum Ausruhen zu schaffen.

A COVERED PERGOLA produces different scenes of light and shadow that can be emphasized by artisan elements with rough textures, producing a warm environment throughout the day. Floor covering can be used to delimitate each area of the terrace according to its function.

UNA CUBIERTA PERGOLADA, produce a lo largo del día diferentes escenas de luz y sombra que pueden ser enfatizadas por elementos artesanales con texturas rugosas produciendo un ambiente cálido. El recubrimiento del piso puede delimitar cada zona de la terraza acorde a su función.

UNE TOITURE EN FORME DE PERGOLA produit tout au long de la journée des scènes de lumière différentes et des ombres qui peuvent être soulignées par des éléments d'artisanat ayant des textures rugueuses qui produisent une ambiance accueillante. Le revêtement du plancher peut délimiter chaque zone de la terrasse selon sa fonction.

EIN PERGOLAGLEICHES DACH produziert im Verlaufe des Tages unterschiedliche Szenerien aus Licht und Schatten, die durch kunsthandwerkliche Elemente mit rauen Texturen betont werden können, somit ein warmes Ambiente schaffend. Der Bodenbelag kann jeden Bereich der Terrasse gemäss seiner Funktion abgrenzen.

# city
# ciudad
# ville
# stadt

UNIFYING THE GEOMETRIC LANGUAGE of the entire façade allows us to appreciate it as an organized and visually clean unit. Changes in floor levels as well as projections of flared roofs and windows will produce volumetrically interesting shadows that will be highlighted by using neutral colors on the walls. The presence of vegetation and natural stones reduce the harshness of a sober façade.

UNIFICAR EL LENGUAJE GEOMÉTRICO de toda la fachada permite apreciarla como una unidad ordenada y visualmente limpia. Los cambios de nivel en pisos así como las proyecciones de cubiertas o ventanas abocinadas producirán sombras volumétricamente interesantes que serán resaltadas al emplear colores neutros en los muros. La presencia de vegetación y piedras naturales reducen la dureza de una fachada sobria.

UNIFIER LE LANGAGE GÉOMÉTRIQUE de toute la façade permet de l'apprécier comme une unité ordonnée et visuellement propre. Les changements de niveau par étages, ainsi que les projections des couvertures ou fenêtres en forme de pavillon produiront des ombres intéressantes du point de vue volumétrique qu'on rehaussera avec des couleurs neutres pour el murs. La présence de végétation et de pierre naturelle adoucit la dureté d'une façade sobre.

DEN GEOMETRISCHEN AUSDRUCK der gesamten Fassade zu vereinheitlichen, erlaubt es sie als eine geordnete, optische reine, Einheit zu würdigen. Die verschiedenen Ebenen der Etagen, sowie die Projektionen der Dächer oder der ausgetellten Fenster produzieren Schatten, die durch die neutralen Farben der Mauern hervorgehoben werden. Die Präsenz von Pflanzen und Natursteinen mindert die Härte einer nüchternen Fassade.

façades fachadas façades fassaden

ONE OF THE BEST WAYS to highlight the gantry access design is to unify the material that will be used in it by extending it as if it were a single piece that covers the floor and culminates in the highest part of the façade. You. must aware of the proportions, and windows can serve as reference.

UNA DE LAS MEJORES FORMAS de resaltar el diseño de nuestro pórtico de acceso es unificar el material que emplearemos en él extendiéndolo como si fuera una sola pieza que recorre el piso y culmina en la parte más alta de la fachada. Debe cuidarse la proporción, las ventanas pueden servirnos de referencia.

UNE DES MEILLEURES FAÇONS de souligner le design de notre portique d'accès est unifier le matériel qu'on y utilise en l'étendant comme si c'était une seule pièce qui parcourt le sol et culmine dans la partie la plus élevée de la façade. Il faut soigner la proportion, les fenêtres peuvent nous servir de référence.

EINE SEHR GUTE ART das Design des Eingangsbereiches zu betonen, ist es das verwendete Material zu vereinheitlichen und es wie ein einziges Stück, das den Boden entlangführt und im höchsten Punkt der Fassade endet, auszubreiten. Man muss auf die Proportionen achten, wobei die Fenster als Referenz dienen können.

The pointed horizontality of the façade is balanced with a portico at double-height that contains a small stone garden and a mirror of water. The tree brings character and solemnity to the space.

La acentuada horizontalidad de la fachada es equilibrada con un pórtico a doble altura que contiene un pequeño jardín pétreo y un espejo de agua. El árbol presente imprime carácter y solemnidad al espacio.

Le caractère très horizontal de la façade est équilibré par un portique à double hauteur qui contient un petit jardin de pierre et un miroir d'eau. La présence de l'arbre imprime de la personnalité et solennité à l'espace.

Die betont horizontale Fassade wird durch ein Portal in doppelter Höhe ausgeglichen, in dem sich ein kleiner Steingarten und ein Wasserspiegel befinden. Der Baum prägt den Bereich mit Charakter und Festlichkeit.

AS WELL AS BEING THE FACE of our home, the façade is also the architectural representation of the shelter; it represents the privacy and the physical boundary between our personal space and public space. To fulfill this purpose, its design can be based on the use of double-height walls without openings or windows.

UNA FACHADA ADEMÁS DE SER el rostro de nuestro hogar es también la representación arquitectónica del resguardo, la privacidad y el límite físico entre nuestro espacio personal y el espacio común de la ciudad. Para cumplir tal finalidad, su diseño puede fundamentarse en el uso de muros de doble altura sin vanos o ventanas.

UNE FAÇADE N'EST PAS SEULEMENT le visage de notre maison, mais aussi la représentation architectonique de l'abri, la vie privée et la limite physique entre notre espace personnel et l'espace en commun de la ville. Pour cela, son design peut être fondé sur des murs à double hauteur sans embrasures ni fenêtres.

EINE FASSADE, ABGESEHEN davon dass sie das Gesicht unseres Hauses ist, ist auch die architektonische Darstellung des Heimes, des Privaten und der physischen Grenze zwischen unserem persönlichen Bereich und dem öffentlichen Bereich der Stadt. Um dieses Ziel zu erreichen, kann man ein Design wählen, das auf Mauern in doppelter Höhe ohne Öffnungen oder Fenster basiert.

WHEN WE ALLOW THE MODULATION of the materials or the construction systems to be partially visible, we create a more avant-garde and daring image of our façade. The sobriety of the colors, a select palette of materials and the low height of the vegetation favors the appreciation of the whole set of lines that form part of the architectural design.

HACER PARCIALMENTE VISIBLE la modulación de los materiales o los sistemas constructivos empleados nos otorgará una imagen más vanguardista y audaz de nuestra fachada. La sobriedad de los colores, una selecta paleta de materiales y la baja altura de la vegetación favorecerá la apreciación visual de todo el conjunto de líneas que forman parte del diseño arquitectónico.

LA VISIBILITÉ PARTIELLE de la modulation des matériaux ou des systèmes de construction nous donnera une image plus avant-garde et audacieuse de notre façade. La sobriété des couleurs, une palette choisie de matériaux et une végétation basse favorisent l'appréciation visuelle de tout l'ensemble des lignes qui forment le design architectural.

DIE FORMGEBUNG DER MATERIALIEN ODER DIE ANGEWENDETE Bauweise teilweilse sichtbar zu machen, gewährt uns eine avantgardistischeres und kühneres Bild unserer Fassade. Die Schlichtheit der Farben, eine ausgesuchte Auswahl an Materialien und die niedrige Bepflanzung begünstigen die optische Würdigung der Linien, die zusammen das architektonische Design ausmachen.

WHEN THE DESIGN OF THE HOUSE does not have too much volume in its entirety, it is preferable to resort to the use of floor-to-ceiling windows, as this allows for a greater appreciation of, and visual contact with the outside landscape design, which may include a mirror of water, a stone rug or a green wall.

CUANDO EL DISEÑO DE LA CASA no posee demasiada volumetría en su lenguaje formal es preferible recurrir al uso de ventanales de piso a techo para tener mayor apreciación y contacto visual con el diseño de paisaje de las zonas exteriores, las cuales pueden incluir un espejo de agua, un tapete pétreo o un muro verde.

QUAND LE DESIGN DE LA MAISON ne possède pas trop de volumétrie dans son langage formel, il vaut mieux avoir recours aux grandes fenêtres du plafond au plancher pour avoir une meilleure appréciation et un bon contact visuel avec le design du paysage des espaces extérieurs, qui peuvent inclure un miroir d'eau, un tapis de pierre ou un mur vert.

WENN DAS DESIGN DES HAUSES in seinem formellen Ausdruck nicht zu voluminös angelegt ist, sollte man lieber auf auf Wandfenster vom Boden bis zum Dach zurückgreifen, um das Design der Landschaft im Aussenbereich, das einen Wasserspiegel, einen Steinteppich oder eine begrünte Mauer enthalten kann, besser würdigen und besser mit ihm in optischem Kontakt stehen zu können.

THE FAÇADE HAS BEEN DESIGNED taking into consideration the duality between the hermetic space of the private area and the maximum transparency of the public area of the house. This way, a harmonious relationship is created between the lighting design, the warmth of the wood, and both the internal and external spatial extent of the whole unit. Keeping and incorporating the existing tree to the interior space is a gesture which aesthetically enriches the entire façade design.

LA FACHADA HA SIDO DISEÑADA a través de la dualidad entre el espacio hermético de la zona privada y la transparencia máxima de la zona pública de la casa. Así, entran en armónica relación el diseño de iluminación, la calidez de las maderas y la amplitud espacial tanto interna como externa de todo el conjunto. Conservar e incorporar el árbol existente al espacio interior es un gesto que enriquece estéticamente el diseño de toda la fachada.

ON A ACHEVÉ LE DESIGN DE LA FAÇADE au moyen de la dualité entre l'espace hermétique de la zone privée et la transparence maximale de la zone publique de la maison. Il y a ainsi une relation harmonieuse entre le design de l'éclairage, la chaleur des bois et l'amplitude spatiale, aussi bien interne qu'externe, de l'ensemble. Conserver et incorporer l'arbre à l'espace intérieur est un geste qui enrichi esthétiquement le design de toute la façade.

DIE FASSADE WURDE BASIEREND auf der Dualität zwischen dem abgeschlossene privatem Bereich und der maximalen Tranzparenz des öffentlichen Bereiches des Hauses, entworfen. So wird eine harmonische Beziehung zwischen dem Beleuchtungsdesign, der Wärme des Holzes und der räumlichen Weite, sowohl im Innen- als auch im Aussenbereich, geschaffen. Den bereits vorhandenen Baum zu bewahren und ihn in den Innenbereich zu integrieren ist eine Geste, die ästhetisch das Design der gesamten Fassade bereichert.

THE PRESENCE OF THREE FACTORS is elemental to create a captivating and impressive façade: the balanced use of light (natural or artificial), the discrete presence of vegetation or stone elements, and the correct selection of materials to harmonize the hues, shapes and textures present in the façade.

LA PRESENCIA DE TRES FACTORES es elemental para lograr una fachada cautivadora e impactante: el equilibrado uso de la luz (natural o artificial), la discreta presencia de vegetación o elementos pétreos y la selección correcta de materiales para armonizar educadamente las tonalidades, las formas y las texturas presentes.

LA PRÉSENCE DE TROIS FACTEURS est élémentaire pour réussir une façade séduisante et impressionnante : l'usage équilibré de la lumière (naturelle ou artificielle), la présence discrète de la végétation ou d'éléments de pierre, et la sélection correcte de matériaux pour harmoniser savamment les tonalités, les formes et les textures.

DREI FAKTOREN sind fundamental, um eine packende und eindrucksvolle Fassade zu schaffen: die ausgewogene Nutzung des Lichts (natürlich und künstlich), die diskrete Präsenz von Pflanzen oder Steinelementen und die richtige Auswahl des Materials, um die Farbtöne, die Formen und die Texturen in Harmonie zu bringen.

swimming pools • piscinas • piscines • schwimmbecken

THE VENETIAN MOSAIC is one of the preferred materials for coating pools. Its variety of colors, shapes and even patterns also make it a versatile, reliable and lasting option that requires minimal maintenance, which represents low costs.

EL MOSAICO VENECIANO es uno de los materiales consentidos para recubrir las albercas. Su variedad de colores, formas e incluso patrones hacen que sea además de versátil una opción confiable y duradera que exige mantenimiento mínimo representando bajo costo.

LA MOSAÏQUE est un des matériaux préférés pour revêtir les piscines. La variété de ses couleurs, ses formes, et même ses schémas en fait non seulement une option versatile, mais aussi fiable et durable, qui exige un minimum d'entretien, et donc représente un coût modeste.

VENEZIANISCHES MOSAIK ist eines der bevorzugten Materialien für die Auskleidung von Schwimmbecken. Die Auswahl an Farben, Formen und Mustern macht es nicht nur vielseitig, sondern auch zu einer verlässlichen und dauerhaften Option, die nur minimale Pflege erfordert und damit geringe Kosten verursacht.

YOU CAN BE MUCH BOLDER and customize the layout of a pool by using a range of colors in the lighting. The area is constantly transformed according to the time of day and night, allowing us to experience environments with different atmospheres (intimate, casual, etc).

SE PUEDE SER MUCHO MÁS AUDAZ y personalizar el diseño de una piscina a través de la gama de colores usada en la iluminación. Estos espacios se transforman conforme el día y la noche llegan a ellos, nuestra percepción se modifica permitiendo ambientes con una atmósfera más íntima o extrovertida según el momento del día.

ON PEUT ÊTRE BEAUCOUP PLUS AUDACIEUX et personnaliser le design d'une piscine au moyen de la gamme de couleurs qu'on utilise pour l'éclairage. Ces espaces se transforment à mesure qu'ils sont atteints par le jour et la nuit, notre perception se modifie permettant des ambiances à l'atmosphère plus intime ou extrovertie selon le moment de la journée.

MAN KANN SEHR VIEL KÜHNER sein und das Design eines Schwimmbeckens, durch die Farbpalette in der benutzten Beleuchtung, persönlich gestalten. Solche Bereiche verändern sich im Verlaufe des Tages oder des Abends, unsere Wahrnehmung verändert sich und erlaubt, vom Zeitpunkt abhängend, eine intimere oder extrovertiertere Atmosphäre.

Bodies of water are large scale architectural mirrors: their ornamental function is to amplify the area and double its aesthetic qualities.

Los cuerpos de agua son espejos arquitectónicos de gran escala: amplificar el espacio y duplicar sus cualidades estéticas son parte de su función ornamental.

Les bassins sont des miroirs architectoniques à grande échelle : amplifier l'espace et doubler ses qualités esthétiques font partie de leur fonction ornementale.

Wasserkörper sind grosse architektonische Spiegel: den Raum zu erweitern und seine ästhetischen Eigenschaften zu verdoppeln, sind Teil seiner dekorativen Funktion.

THE DESIGN OF A POOL should never be solemn. On the contrary, it should be fun, joyful, and festive, yet always elegant. By using the colors of the coatings and taking them with certain variations of tone to the interior design of the closest spaces will lead to a fresh and relaxed image which can be strengthened by including works of art or furniture with the same range of colors.

EL DISEÑO DE UNA PISCINA nunca debe ser solemne, por el contrario debe ser muy divertida, alegre, un espacio festivo sin dejar de lado la elegancia. Emplear de forma evidente los colores de los recubrimientos de ésta y llevarlos con ciertas variaciones de tono al diseño interior de los espacios más cercanos propiciará una imagen fresca y relajada, la cual se puede reforzar al incluir obras de arte o mobiliario con la misma gama de colores.

LE DESIGN D'UNE PISCINE ne doit jamais être solennel, mais au contraire, elle doit être très amusante, joyeuse, un espace de fête, qui ne laisse cependant pas l'élégance de côté. Employer de façon évidente les couleurs de son revêtement et les porter avec quelques variations de ton au design intérieur des espaces les plus proches favorisera une image fraîche et détendue, qui peut être renforcée par l'inclusion d'œuvres d'art ou de mobilier ayant la même gamme de couleurs.

DAS DESIGN EINES SCHWIMMBECKENS darf nie zu ernst sein, im Gegenteil, es sollte Spass machen, fröhlich sein, ein Ort zum feiern, ohne Eleganz zu verlieren. Die starke Farbe der Verkleidung und diese mit leichten Änderungen im Ton in das Innendesign der angrenzenden Bereiche zu tragen, schafft ein frisches und entspanntes Bild, das noch durch Kunstwerke oder Möbel im gleichen Farbspektrum verstärkt werden kann.

BY GIVING UP THE TRADITION of constructing a rectangular pool, you will be able to build a much more attractive and interesting area using designs based on organic forms and free range. And by adding drops of water and making sure that the lounge chairs or other furniture have the same formal language, you will give the area personality and character and avoid a monotonous design.

RENUNCIAR A LA TRADICIÓN de construir una alberca rectangular hará que un diseño basado en formas orgánicas y de carácter libre sea mucho más atractivo e interesante para sus usuarios. Añadir caídas de agua y vigilar que los camastros u otros muebles tengan el mismo lenguaje formal dotará de personalidad y carácter el espacio, evitando caer en lo monótono.

SI L'ON RENONCE À LA TRADITION de construire une piscine rectangulaire on aura un design basé sur des formes organiques et un caractère libre qui sera beaucoup plus attrayant et intéressant pour ses usagers. Ajouter des chutes d'eau et veiller à ce que les chaises longues et autres meubles aient le même langage formel complètera la personnalité et le caractère de l'espace, en évitant sombrer dans la monotonie.

DIE TRADITION AUFZUGEBEN rechteckige Schwimmbecken zu bauen, lässt ein auf organischen Formen beruhendes und freieres Design sehr viel attraktiver und interessanter für die Benutzer werden. Wasserfälle beizufügen und darauf zu achten, dass Liegen und andere Möbel den gleichen formellen Ausdruck haben, gibt dem Bereich Persönlichkeit und Charakter und vermeidet in Monotonie zu verfallen.

A swimming pool can become the main attraction of a residence because of its elegance and its capacity to highlight the lines of the architectural design regardless of whether your style is classic or contemporary. The contrast in colors and materials should be considerably accentuated.

Una alberca puede convertirse en la principal atracción de una residencia por su elegancia y manera de resaltar las líneas del diseño arquitectónico sin importar si su estilo es clásico o contemporáneo. El contraste en colores y materiales debe acentuarse considerablemente.

Une piscine peut devenir la principale attraction d'une résidence par son élégance et sa façon de rehausser les lignes du design architectural, qu'elle soit de style classique ou contemporain. Le contraste en couleurs et matériaux doit être considérablement accentué.

Ein Schwimmbecken kann durch seine Eleganz und die Art, wie durch die Linienführung das architektonische Design herausgestellt wird, zur Hauptattraktion einer Residenz werden, wobei es nicht wichtig ist, ob der Stil klassisch oder zeitgenössisch is,. Der Kontrast der Farben und Materialien sollte deutlich betont werden.

terraces
terrazas
terrasses
terrassen

WITH THE ARRIVAL OF SUMMER, a terrace in the city becomes one of the most pleasant places to enjoy the comfort of your home. Spending long and comfortable rest sessions at the terrace will allow us to pamper all our senses through a connection with nature, while isolating them from the urban environment.

CON LA LLEGADA DEL VERANO, una terraza en la ciudad se convierte en uno de los espacios más agradables para disfrutar en la comodidad del hogar. Pasar largas y confortables sesiones de descanso es una estupenda oportunidad para consentir todos nuestros sentidos vinculándolos con la naturaleza o aislándolos del entorno urbano.

QUAND ARRIVE L'ÉTÉ, une terrasse en ville devient un des espaces les plus agréables pour profiter du confort de la maison. Vivre de longues séances de repos confortable est une excellente opportunité pour gâter tous nos sens en les rapprochant de la nature ou les isolant de l'ambiance urbaine.

MIT DEM BEGINN DES SOMMERS wird eine Terrasse in der Stadt zu einem dem angenehmsten Ort um die Bequemlichkeiten des Heimes su geniessen. Lange und bequeme Ruhezeiten sind eine hervorragende Möglichkeit unsere Sinne zu verwöhnen, indem wir sie mit der Natur verbinden oder sie von der städtischen Umgebung fernhalten.

THE LACK OF DECORATIVE ELEMENTS is an ideal alternative for visually neat terraces or terraces whose function is completely defined, such as room, dining room or lounge area. However, if such functions are combined freely in the same space, it is worth enriching it by adding objects of ornamental character with tonalities that correspond harmoniously with the floors, walls or soffits.

PRESCINDIR DE ELEMENTOS DECORATIVOS es una alternativa ideal para terrazas visualmente pulcras o donde su función esté totalmente definida, por ejemplo como sala, comedor o área de descanso. Sin embargo, si tales funciones se conjugan de forma libre en un mismo espacio, vale la pena enriquecerlo añadiendo objetos de carácter ornamental que correspondan armoniosamente con sus tonalidades a los pisos, muros o plafones.

SE PASSER D'ÉLÉMENTS DÉCORATIFS est une alternative idéale pour les terrasses visuellement dépouillées ou bien là où leur fonction est absolument définie, comme, par exemple, le salon, la salle à manger ou la zone de repos. Cependant, si ces fonctions se conjuguent librement dans un même espace, ça vaut la peine de l'enrichir en ajoutant des objets d'ornement dont les tonalités correspondent harmonieusement aux planchers, les murs ou les plafonds.

AUF DEKORATION ZU VERZICHTEN ist eine ideale Alternative für optisch reine Terrassen oder wo ihre Funktion deutlich definiert ist, zum Beispiel als Wohnbereich, Essbereich oder Ruhezone. Wenn jedoch diese Funktionen in freier Form in dem selben Bereich verbunden sind, ist es der Mühe wert dekorative Stücke zu ergänzen, die in ihren Farbtönen harmonisch zu den Böden, Wänden und Decken passen.

When you incorporate one or more pots you must ask yourself which of them is more suitable for the type of plant you wish to use, taking into account the climate or the specific place that it will occupy on the terrace.

Al incorporar una o más macetas debes preguntarte cuál es la que más favorece al tipo de planta que deseas contener tomando en cuenta el clima o lugar específico que ocupará en la terraza.

Quand on incorpore un ou deux pots de fleurs, on doit se demander quelle est le meilleur pour le type de plante que l'on veut avoir, tenant compte du climat ou l'endroit spécifique qu'elle occupera dans la terrasse.

Bei der Verwendung von einem oder mehreren Pflanztöpfen, muss man sich fragen welche für die gewünschten Pflanzen angemessen sind und sollte dabei das Klima und den spezifischen Standort auf der Terrasse bedenken.

IF WE HAVE A REDUCED SPACE to be used as a terrace, it is imperative to consider the location of the furniture and its dimensions. Directing them towards the areas of greatest visual interest and ensuring that they have narrow or low rests, so as not to reduce the field of vision, is one of the best solutions for this scenario.

SI CONTAMOS CON UN ESPACIO REDUCIDO para habilitarlo como terraza será sustancial considerar la ubicación de los muebles y sus dimensiones. Dirigirlos hacia las zonas de mayor interés visual, así como vigilar que éstos cuenten con respaldos angostos o de baja altura para no reducir el campo visual, es uno de los mejores recursos al que se puede apelar.

SI NOUS N'AVONS QU'UN ESPACE RÉDUIT pour l'habiliter comme terrasse, il est important de penser à la disposition des meubles, ainsi qu'à leurs dimensions. Les diriger vers les espaces ayant un plus grand intérêt visuel, ainsi que veiller à ce qu'ils aient un dossier étroit ou bas, pour ne pas réduire le champ visuel, est une des meilleures solutions.

WENN WIR EINEN EHER KLEINEN BEREICH für die Terrasse zur Verfügung haben, ist es wichtig die Anordnung der Möbel und ihre Grösse zu bedenken. Sie auf die Zonen, die optisch am interessantesten sind, auszurichten, sowie darauf zu achten, dass die Rückenlehnen schmal und von niedriger Höhe sind um nicht das Sichtfeld zu reduzieren, ist eine der besten Mittel zu denen man greifen kann.

CONCRETE, BEING a cold material, can be combined with woods in light colors, and the furniture may include curved strokes to break the rigidity of the architectural elements. You can make this area much more glamorous by incorporating a flowerbed - painted with the same color as the dividers-containing seasonal plants that will provide this space with personality and life.

EL CONCRETO APARENTE por ser un material frío puede combinarse con maderas en tonos claros y el mobiliario puede incluir trazos curvos para romper la rigidez de los elementos arquitectónicos. Hacer mucho más encantadora esta área puede lograrse a través de la presencia de un arriate -pintado con el mismo color de la cancelería- conteniendo plantas estacionales que ponderarán el paso del tiempo, dotando de personalidad y vida este espacio.

LE BÉTON APPARENT, étant un matériel froid, peut être combiné avec les bois aux tons clairs et le mobilier peut inclure des traits courbés pour briser la rigidité des éléments architecturaux. On peut avoir une zone beaucoup plus charmante avec une plate-bande, de la même couleur que les châssis, contenant des plantes de la saison qui mesureront le passage du temps, dotant cet espace de personnalité et de vie.

ZEMENT, da es ein kaltes Material ist, kann mit Holz in hellen Tönen kombiniert werden und die Möbel können kurvige Formen haben, um mit der Steifheit der architektonischen Elemente zu brechen. Dieser Bereich kann mit einem Pflanzkasten – in der gleichen Farbe wie die Türen und Fenster gestrichen – mit Pflanzen der Saison bestückt, die den Verlauf der Zeit aufzeigen, sehr viel charmanter gestaltet werden und sie verleihen dem Bereich Persönlichkeit und Leben.

WHETHER THEY ARE INSIDE OR OUTSIDE, terraces may be part of different atmospheres to create maximum comfort. However, the local climate must be taken into account to determine if it is worthwhile to design it completely open or covered. A fireplace is suitable for colder climates, and it is a classic element that will give us the possibility of spending long nights in this space.

EN EL INTERIOR O EN EL EXTERIOR, las terrazas pueden formar parte de diferentes atmósferas para provocar el máximo confort posible; sin embargo debe tomarse en cuenta el clima local para determinar si vale la pena diseñarla totalmente abierta o a cubierto. Una chimenea adquiere sentido una vez que se ha respondido lo anterior y se desea contar con un elemento clásico que nos brindará la posibilidad de pasar largas sesiones nocturnas.

A L'INTÉRIEUR OU L'EXTÉRIEUR, les terrasses peuvent faire partie de diverses ambiances pour créer le plus de confort possible ; cependant, on doit prendre en compte le climat local pour décider s'il vaut mieux les concevoir totalement ouvertes ou couvertes. La cheminée acquiert un sens une fois qu'on a résolu cette question et on veut avoir un élément classique qui nous donnera la possibilité d'y passer de longues sessions nocturnes.

IM INNEN- ODER AUSSENBEREICH, Terrassen können Teil unterschiedlicher Atmosphären sein, um den grösstmöglichen Komfort zu bieten; ohne Zweifel muss man das örtliche Klima bedenken, um zu entscheiden, ob es sich lohnt, sie vollständig offen oder überdacht zu planen. Eine Feuerstelle macht Sinn, wenn man diese Frage beantwortet hat und man auf ein klassisches Element zählen möchte, das uns die Möglichkeit gibt dort lange nächtliche Stunden zu verbringen.

A terrace in the city can give you a unique privilege if you design it as an intimate vantage point, as it will serve as a platform to observe urban life for short periods of time if it has a panoramic view.

Una terraza dentro de la ciudad puede ser un privilegio único al diseñarla como un mirador íntimo, una plataforma para observar la vida urbana por breves lapsos de tiempo si se cuenta con una panorámica singular.

Une terrasse dans la ville peut être un privilège unique si on la conçoit comme un belvédère intime, une plateforme pour observer la vie urbaine pendant quelques minutes si on a une vue panoramique singulière.

Eine Terrasse in der Stadt kann ein einmaliges Privileg sein, wenn man sie als einen intimen Aussichtspunkt entwirft, eine Plattform, um das städtische Leben für kurze Zeiten zu beobachen, wenn sie eine einzigartige Aussicht hat.

A TERRACE can reach maximum purity when nothing of ornamental value needs to be showcased in it. For example, a patio with strong similarities to a Zen garden formed exclusively by the beauty of the textures of pavements, the natural colors of the materials used in the façades and the light that fills the space, producing shadows throughout the day. Contrary to what you might think about the waste of space, this style enhances all the qualities of the terrace, creating a silent refuge that is capable of transmitting a feeling of calm and relaxation.

UNA TERRAZA puede llegar a la depuración máxima donde nada de lo ornamental merezca figurar. Por ejemplo, un patio con fuertes similitudes a un jardín zen conformado exclusivamente por la belleza de las texturas de los pavimentos, los colores naturales de los materiales empleados en las fachadas y la luz que colma el espacio produciendo sombras a lo largo del día. Contrario a lo que pueda pensarse sobre el derroche del espacio, en este estilo se realzan todas sus cualidades para obtener un refugio colmado de silencio capaz de trasmitir una sensación de calma y relajación.

UNE TERRASSE peut atteindre une dépuration maximale où rien de ce qui est ornemental ne mérite d'y figurer. Par exemple, un patio qui ressemble fortement a un jardin zen formé exclusivement par la beauté des textures des pavés, les couleurs naturelles des matériaux employés pour les façades et la lumière qui remplit l'espace produisant des ombres pendant toute la journée. Contrairement à ce qu'on pourrait penser quand au gâchis d'espace, ce style souligne toutes ses qualités pour obtenir un refuge plein de silence capable de transmettre une sensation de calme et de détente.

EINE TERRASSE kann maximale Reinheit erreichen, in der keinerlei Schmuck einen Platz verdient. Zum Beispiel, ein Hof mit starker Ähnlichkeit zu einem Zen Garten, der ausschliesslich aus der Schönheit der Texturen des Bodens, den natürlichen Farben der für die Fassade benutzten Materialien und dem Licht besteht, das den Bereich erfüllt, im Verlauf des Tages Schatten produzierend. Im Gegenteil zu dem Gedanken, dass man diesen Bereich verschwendet, werden in diesem Stil alle Qualitäten hervorgehoben, um eine Zuflucht zu schaffen, mit Stille erfüllt, die fähig ist, ein Gefühl von Ruhe und Entspannung zu vermitteln.

THE AREAS THAT CAN FUNCTION as terraces tend to be small in the city due to the design of apartments or houses, which are frequently of minimum dimensions. The foregoing may represent one major challenge to style it up and get optimal results. However, you can overcome this obstacle by doing the following: decorate or add vegetation to existing balconies, do not use furniture that is too large, and make sure that these can be versatile and are of simple geometric shape.

LOS ESPACIOS QUE PUEDEN FUNCIONAR como terrazas suelen ser pequeños en la ciudad debido al diseño de departamentos o casas de dimensiones mínimas. Lo anterior puede representar un desafío mayor para ambientarlo y obtener óptimos resultados; sin embargo puede lograrse exaltando los siguientes aspectos: decorar o añadir vegetación a balcones existentes, no seleccionar muebles demasiado grandes y procurar que estos puedan ser versátiles y de trazos geométricos sobrios.

LES ESPACES POUVANT FONCTIONNER en tant que terrasses sont généralement réduits dans la ville, à cause des petites dimensions des appartements ou des maisons. Ceci peut représenter un défi encore plus grand quand il s'agit de leur donner une ambiance avec les meilleurs résultats ; cependant, on peut réussir en exaltant les aspects suivants : décorer les balcons existants ou y ajouter des plantes, ne pas choisir des meubles trop grands et faire tout le possible pour qu'ils soient versatiles et aient des traits géométriques sobres.

BEREICHE DIE ALS TERRASSEN DIENEN KÖNNEN, sind in der Stadt oft klein, aufgrund des Designs von Wohnungen oder Häusern minimaler Grösse. Das kann eine grössere Herausforderung darstellen, um sie zu gestalten und optimale Ergebnisse zu erzielen; man kann das jedoch erreichen, indem man folgende Aspekte betont: vorhandene Balkone dekorieren oder Pflanzen hinzufügen, nicht zu grosse Möbel wählen und sicherstellen, dass sie vielseitig und von schlichter geometrischer Form sind.

IT IS WORTH CONSIDERING at all times that a terrace is not a residual space; for this reason, it should be clear that its frequency of use depends on its distance from the meeting areas of a house and the accessibility to the space. If it is situated near the living area, it is beneficial to convert it into an area that is always useful. In contrast, if the distance to access the terrace is substantial and there are no visual stimuli, the space might not be used as often as you would like.

VALE LA PENA CONSIDERAR en todo momento que una terraza no es un espacio residual; por ello, debe tenerse claro que su frecuencia de uso depende de la distancia existente entre las zonas de reunión de una casa y la accesibilidad al espacio. Si su cercanía es menor a las zonas de estar favorecerá a convertir la terraza en un espacio siempre útil. En cambio si para acceder a ésta la distancia se incrementa y no hay estímulos visuales de interés puede provocar que el espacio no se use con la periodicidad deseable.

IL FAUT TOUJOURS PRENDRE EN CONSIDÉRATION qu'une terrasse n'est pas un espace résiduel ; c'est pour cela qu'on doit se rendre compte clairement que la fréquence de son utilisation dépend de la distance entre les zones de réunion dans une maison et l'accessibilité de cet espace. Si la distance entre celle-ci et les zones de séjour est moindre, la terrasse deviendra plus facilement un espace toujours utile. En revanche, si pour y accéder la distance est plus grande, et il n'y a pas de stimulation visuelle intéressante, il se peut que l'espace ne soit pas utilisé autant qu'il serait désirable.

ES LOHNT SICH ZU BEDENKEN, dass eine Terrasse kein zweitrangiger Bereich ist; daher sollte man sich bewusst sein, dass die Häufigkeit ihrer Nutzung von der Entfernung zwischen den Wohnbereichen eines Hauses und ihrem Zugang abhängt. Wenn sie nah an den Wohnbereichen ist, ist es einfacher sie in einen immer praktischen Bereich zu verwandeln. Wenn aber die Entfernung grösser ist und es keine intelerssanten optischen Reize auf ihr gibt, kann es passieren, dass der Bereich nicht in der gewünschten Weise genutzt wird.

COMFORT AND RELAXATION are the main attributes of a bright, fresh and modern terrace. The style, personality and taste of the user can be emphasized by using marble covers in the outer table, as well as with the presence of accessories that are used frequently, such as a grill. If it is necessary to consider subdivisions between existing zones, you should resort preferably to transparent or folding elements that allow you to keep eye contact with the entire area at all times, and which do not represent visual obstacles.

LA COMODIDAD Y LA RELAJACIÓN son los principales atributos de una terraza luminosa, fresca y vanguardista. El estilo, la personalidad y gusto del usuario pueden ser acentuados empleando cubiertas de mármol en la mesa exterior así como contando con la presencia de accesorios de uso frecuente como un asador. Si es necesario plantear subdivisiones entre las zonas existentes debe recurrirse preferentemente a elementos transparentes o plegables que permitan mantener en todo momento contacto visual con toda el área y que no representen obstáculos visuales.

LE CONFORT ET LA DÉTENTE sont les principales attributions d'une terrasse lumineuse, fraîche et avant-garde. Le style, la personnalité et le goût de l'usager peuvent être accentués en employant des couvertures en marbre pour la table de l'extérieur et avec la présence d'accessoires à usage fréquent, tels qu'un barbecue. S'il faut établir des sous-divisions dans les zones existantes, il vaut mieux utiliser des éléments transparents ou pliables qui puissent préserver à tout moment le contact visuel avec tout l'espace et qui ne représentent pas d'obstacles visuels.

BEQUEMLICHKEIT UND ENTSPANNUNG sind die Hauptmerkmale einer hellen Terrasse, frisch und avantgardistisch. Der Stil, die Persönlichkeit und der Geschmack der Benutzer können durch eine Marmorplatte auf dem Tisch draussen betont werden und durch oft benutzte Elemente wie einem Grill. Wenn es notwendig ist die verschiedenen Zonen zu unterteilen, sollte man vorzugsweise auf durchsichtige oder faltbare Elemente zurückgreifen, die es erlauben immer in optischem Kontakt mit dem gesamten Bereich zu stehen und die kein optisches Hinterniss darstellen.

THE SELECTION OF FURNITURE for the terrace should be based on the following aspects: dimensions, utility, quality of the materials and, of course, style. Since this last factor is an exclusively personal decision, it is possible to be bold and audacious with the variations in the colors and shapes. If the area possesses ochre tones, a vibrant tone is an excellent alternative.

LA SELECCIÓN DE MUEBLES para la terraza debe realizarse en función de los siguientes aspectos: dimensiones, utilidad, calidad en los materiales y, por supuesto, el estilo. Siendo este último factor una decisión exclusivamente personal es posible recurrir con audacia a variaciones en los colores y las formas de cada uno de ellos. Si el ambiente posee tonos ocres, un tono vibrante es una excelente alternativa.

LE CHOIX DES MEUBLES pour la terrasse doit se faire en fonction des aspects suivants: dimensions, utilité, qualité des matériaux, et, bien sûr, le style. Ce dernier point étant une décision exclusivement personnelle, on peut avoir l'audace de faire des variations avec les couleurs et les formes de chacun d'entre eux. Si l'ambiance possède des tons ocre, un ton vibrant est une excellente option.

DIE AUSWAHL DER MÖBEL für die Terrasse sollte nach folgenden Kriterien erfolgen: Grösse, Nutzbarkeit, Qualität des Materials und selbstverständlich dem Stil. Letzteres ist ausschliesslich eine persönliche Entscheidung und es ist möglich kühn verschiedene Farben und Formen zu wählen. Wenn das Ambiente von Ockertönen geprägt ist, ist eine kräftige Farbe ein guter Kontrast.

OCHRE HUES give a nostalgic look to this terrace, which also includes the presence of a large mud "maceton" and some light bulbs with great rustic personality. The texture of the floor, its discrete geometric patterns in stone, as well as the selection of classic furniture radiate warmth and comfort within a much more serene environment. A touch of color may be appropriate to break the monochromatic look.

TONALIDADES OCRES imprimen un sello nostálgico a esta terraza que además incorpora la presencia de un gran macetón de barro y algunas lamparillas con gran personalidad artesanal. La textura del piso, sus discretos patrones geométricos en piedra así como la selección de muebles de corte clásico irradian calidez y comodidad dentro de un ambiente mucho más sereno. Un toque de color puede ser adecuado para romper la monocromía.

LES TONALITÉS OCRE impriment un sceau nostalgique à cette terrasse, qui incorpore de plus la présence d'un grand pot de fleurs en terre glaise et quelques petites lampes ayant une grande personnalité artisanale. La texture du plancher, ses schémas géométriques discrets en pierre, ainsi que le choix de meubles de style classique rayonnent la chaleur et le confort dans une ambiance beaucoup plus sereine. Une note de couleur peut réussir à briser la monochromie.

OCKERTÖNE prägen dieser Terrasse ein nostalgisches Siegel auf, auf der ausserdem ein grosser Pflanztopf aus Ton und einige Lampen mit kunsthandwerklichem Anstrich zu finden sind. Die Textur des Bodens, seine diskreten geometrischen Muster aus Stein, sowie die Auswahl der klassisch geschnittenen Möbel strahlen Wärme und Komfort innerhalb eines sehr viel kühleren Ambientes aus. Ein Hauch Farbe kann angemessen sein, um die Einfarbigkeit aufzubrechen.

WHEN YOU SELECT DIFFERENT chairs that have completely different and opposing designs, you can create a feel of playfulness in the area without necessarily fall into undesirable saturation. To achieve this it is common to use vivid colors, antique or contemporary styles. And you must ensure that the dimensions of the space are suited to allow circulation, ensuring the desired comfort.

SELECCIONAR DIFERENTES SILLAS que posean un lenguaje en su diseño totalmente opuesto entre sí, puede generar un espacio de carácter lúdico sin que necesariamente caiga en una saturación indeseable. Para lograrlo es común emplear colores vivos, estilos antiguos o contemporáneos y vigilar las dimensiones del espacio para permitir adecuadamente la circulación garantizando la comodidad o el confort deseado al estar en él.

CHOISIR DES CHAISES DIFFÉRENTES ayant un langage de design tout-à-fait opposé peut générer un espace à caractère ludique sans tomber nécessairement dans une saturation non souhaitable. Pour réussir, on emploie en général des couleurs vives, des styles anciens ou contemporains, et on contrôle les dimensions de l'espace pour permettre une circulation appropriée qui garantit le confort que l'on y cherche.

UNTERSCHIEDLICHE STÜHLE ZU WÄHLEN, die einen vollkommen gegensätzlichen Ausdruck in ihrem Design haben, kann einen Bereich mit einem verspieltem Charakter schaffen, ohne in ungewollte Übersättigung zu verfallen. Um das zu erreichen, sollte man lebendige Farben, antiken oder zeitgenössischen Stil, wählen und auf die Grösse des Bereiches achten, um Bewegungsfreiheit zu erlauben und damit die gewünschten Annehmlichkeiten und Komfort bei ihrer Nutzung zu garantieren.

beach
playa
plage
strand

façades
fachadas
façades
fassaden

THE FAÇADE IS THE PRESENTATION CARD of a beach house, and also the first visual message of peace and tranquility that one receives. The palette of materials that can be included in the design of the façade favor wood and nautical colors (white, blue, green), as well as ornamental elements with marine motifs. It is worth mentioning that the stone coatings that are employed must have the quality of being resistant to humidity and corrosion.

UNA FACHADA ES LA CARTA DE PRESENTACIÓN de toda una casa en la playa pero también puede decirse que es el primer mensaje visual de tranquilidad o descanso que uno puede recibir. La paleta de materiales que se puede incluir en el diseño de la fachada recae en maderas y colores náuticos (blanco, azul, verde), así como en elementos ornamentales con motivos marinos. Vale la pena mencionar que los recubrimientos pétreos empleados deben contar con la cualidad de ser resistentes a la humedad y la corrosión.

UNE FAÇADE EST LA LETTRE DE PRÉSENTATION de toute maison de plage, mais on peut dire aussi que c'est le premier message visuel de tranquillité ou repos que l'on peut recevoir. La palette de matériaux qu'on peut inclure dans le design de la façade est formée par les bois et les couleurs nautiques (blanc, bleu, vert), ainsi que par les éléments d'ornement aux motifs maritimes. On peut mentionner que les revêtements en pierre doivent posséder la qualité d'être résistants à l'humidité et la corrosion.

EINE FASSADE IST DIE VISITENKARTE eines jeden Hauses am Strand, aber man kann auch sagen, dass sie die erste optische Botschaft der Stille oder des Ruhens ist, die man empfängt. Die Auswahl der Materialen im Design der Fassade basiert auf Holz und nautischen Farben (Weiss, Blau, Grün), sowie dekorativen Elementen mit Meeresmotiven. Es bleibt zu erwähnen, dass die benutzten Steinabdeckungen die nötige Qualität haben sollten Feuchtigkeit und Korrosion standhalten zu können.

The design of stairs as sculptural elements can generate an interesting game of lights at the different levels of our façade. The latter should always reflect the design of the interiors and the lifestyle of its inhabitants.

El diseño de escaleras como elementos de carácter escultórico puede generar un interesante juego de luces en los diferentes planos de nuestra fachada. Ésta última debe procurar en todo momento ser un reflejo del diseño de interiores y del estilo de vida de sus habitantes.

Le design des escaliers comme des sculptures peut générer un jeu de lumières intéressant sur les différents plans de notre façade. Celle-ci doit chercher à être à tout moment un reflet du design d'intérieurs et le style de vie de ses habitants.

Das Design der Treppen, die wie Skulpturen wirken, kann ein interessantes Lichtspiel auf den verschiedenen Ebenen unserer Fassade verursachen. Die letztere sollte immer ein Widerschein des Innendesigns und des Lebensstils der Bewohner sein.

DEPENDING ON THE LOCATION of our project, we can make formal evocations to old construction systems by using materials and endemic techniques of a site in an innovative manner, as well as artisanal workmanship that endows a particular spirit to a construction.

DEPENDIENDO DE LA UBICACIÓN donde se encuentre nuestro proyecto podemos hacer evocaciones formales a sistemas de construcción antiguos empleando de forma novedosa los materiales y las técnicas endémicas de un sitio, así como la mano de obra artesanal que dotan de un espíritu particular a una construcción.

SELON L'ENDROIT où se trouve notre projet, nous pouvons faire des évocations formelles de systèmes de construction anciens en employant d'une façon nouvelle les matériaux et les techniques propres à un endroit qui donnent un esprit particulier à une construction.

ABHÄNGIG VON DER LAGE unseres Projektes können wir formelle Anspielungen auf antike Konstruktionsweisen machen, indem wir für den Ort typisches Material und Bauweisen in neuer Weise anwenden, sowie kunsthandwerkliche Elemente verwenden, die einem Gebäude eine besondere Energie verleihen.

swimming pools

piscinas

piscines

schwimmbecken

A swimming pool on the beach is perfect to create a relaxed
atmosphere, full of tranquility and harmony. It is not always necessary
to have decorative elements. In fact, in many cases you should
prioritize the possibility of watching the horizon, and for this reason
it is preferable to avoid those objects that may distract our eyes from
something extraordinarily beautiful, worthy of contemplation.

Una piscina en la playa es el acompañante perfecto para alcanzar
un ambiente relajado, colmado de tranquilidad y armonía.
No siempre es necesario tener elementos decorativos, en muchos
casos debe darse prioridad a la posibilidad de observar el horizonte
y por ello es preferible prescindir de aquellos objetos que puedan
distraer nuestra mirada ante algo extraordinariamente bello digno
de contemplación.

Une piscine à la plage est l'accompagnement parfait pour achever
une ambiance détendue, pleine de tranquillité et harmonie. Il n'est
pas toujours nécessaire d'avoir des éléments de décoration, et on
peut souvent accorder la priorité à la possibilité d'observer l'horizon,
et pour cela il vaut mieux se passer des objets qui peuvent distraire
notre regard de quelque chose de si beau et digne de contemplation.

Ein Schwimmbecken am Strand ist eine perfekte Ergänzung um ein
entspanntes Ambiente zu erzielen, erfüllt von Ruhe und Harmonie.
Es ist nicht immer notwendig, dekorative Elemente zu verwenden,
in vielen Fällen muss man der Möglichkeit den Horrizont betrachten
zu können den Vorrang geben und deshalb ist es vorzuziehen auf
Objekte, die unseren Blick von etwas so aussergewöhnlich Schönem
und betrachtenswerten ablenken könnten, zu verzichten.

It is essential to incorporate a plant palette that is heat resistant to frame certain spaces and perspectives from the rest areas. The presence of textures as well as elements that create shadows will make the area much more pleasant.

Es imprescindible incorporar una paleta vegetal resistente al calor que enmarque ciertos espacios y perspectivas desde las zonas de descanso. La presencia de texturas así como de elementos que provoquen sombras logrará convertir el espacio en algo mucho más ameno.

Il est indispensable d'incorporer une palette végétale résistante à la chaleur qui encadre certains espaces et perspectives depuis les zones de repos. La présence de textures ainsi que d'éléments qui provoquent des ombres pourra transformer l'espace en quelque chose de beaucoup plus agréable.

Es ist unverzichtbar eine Auswahl hitzeresistenter Pflanzen mit einzuplanen, die bestimmte Bereiche und von den Ruhezonen ausgehenden Perspektiven einrahmen. Die Präsenz von Texturen, sowie Elementen die Schatten spenden, macht den Bereich sehr viel angenehmer.

THERE ARE MANY NEW TRENDS in swimming pool design and construction, such as the so-called "infinity edge" or swooning shore. This design creates an optical illusion that the pool is perceived as an extension of the sea. The key to achieve the effect is to mirror the color of the sea in the pool, thus achieving a vision and sense of continuity with the horizon.

EXISTEN NUEVAS TENDENCIAS de diseño y construcción de piscinas como la denominada *"infinity edge"* u orilla desvaneciente, en ella se crea una ilusión óptica para que la alberca sea percibida como una extensión del mar. La clave para lograr el efecto está en repetir el color del mar en la alberca, consiguiendo así la visión y sensación de continuidad con el horizonte fusionado.

IL EXISTE DE NOUVELLES TENDANCES en design et construction de piscines, tels que celle qu'on appelle *"infinity edge"* ou bord évanescent, qui crée une illusion optique pour que la piscine soit perçue comme une extension de la mer. La clé pour réussir cet effet est de répéter la couleur de la mer dans la piscine, achevant ainsi la vision et la sensation de continuité avec l'horizon fusionné.

ES GIBT NEUE TENDENZEN im Design und dem Bau von Schwimmbecken, wie die sogannte *"infinity edge"* oder verschwindender Rand, in dem eine optische Illusion geschaffen wird, die das Schwimmbecken als eine Fortführung des Meeres erscheinen lässt. Der Schlüssel um diesen Effekt zu erreichen ist, die Farbe des Meeres im Schwimmbecken zu wiederholen und damit den Eindruck von Fortläufigkeit und ein Verschmelzen mit dem Horrizont zu erreichen.

ANOTHER TREND is to build the access to the pool in a way that mirrors the entrance from the beach to the sea. To succeed in this design you must have an ample access framed by tall palm trees or vegetation. It is necessary to consider the colors and textures (similar to sand) to give this design a greater effect of reality.

OTRA TENDENCIA es la de construir el acceso de la alberca imitando la entrada de la playa al mar, para esto se debe tener un acceso amplio enmarcado por vegetación o palmeras de gran altura. Es necesario considerar los colores y texturas (similares a la arena) para darle a este efecto mayor sensación y efecto de realidad.

UNE AUTRE TENDANCE amène à construire l'accès à la piscine comme une imitation de celle de la plage à la mer ; pour cela on doit avoir un accès ample encadré par de la végétation ou des palmiers assez hauts. Il faut tenir compte des couleurs et des textures (similaires à celles du sable) pour ajouter à la sensation et l'effet de réalité.

EINE ANDERE TENDENZ besteht darin den Zugang zum Schwimmbecken so zu bauen, dass er den Zugang zum Meer am Strand imitiert; dazu sollte es einen weiten Zugang, umrahmt von Pflanzen oder hohen Palmen geben. Es ist notwendig die Farben und Texturen (dem Sand ähnlich)mit Bedacht zu wählen, um diesem Effekt eine stärkere Wirkung und grössere Echtheit zu verleihen.

terraces
terrazas
terrasses
terrassen

A TERRACE TO OBSERVE the sea from can be designed by imagining it as an extension of the architecture towards nature. Its presence must be subtle, almost imperceptible, as it cannot be more attractive than the view you want to contemplate. Evanescence and minimalism can be two of the distinctive features of these spaces, enhanced by the beauty of the natural setting.

UNA TERRAZA PARA OBSERVAR el mar se puede diseñar imaginándola como una extensión de la arquitectura hacia la naturaleza. Su presencia debe ser sutil, casi imperceptible, no puede ser más atractiva que lo que se quiere contemplar, la evanescencia y el minimalismo pueden ser dos de los rasgos distintivos de estos espacios enaltecidos por la belleza de lo existente.

ON PEUT CONCEVOIR UNE TERRASSE pour regarder la mer en l'imaginant comme une extension de l'architecture vers la nature. Sa présence peut être subtile, presque imperceptible, et elle ne peut pas avoir plus d'attrait que ce que l'on veut contempler ; l'évanescence et le minimalisme peuvent être les deux traits distinctifs de ces espaces exaltés par la beauté de la nature.

EINE TERRASSE UM AUF das Meer zu blicken kann man wie eine Fortsetzung der Architektur zur Natur hin planen. Ihre Präsenz sollte subtil, fast unbemerkbar sein, sie kann nicht attraktiver sein, als was man betrachten möchte, Auflösung und Minimalismus können zwei unterschiedliche Merkmale dieser durch die Schönheit des Bestehenden gewürdigten Bereiche sein.

A BEACH HOUSE is primarily a place for social interaction and resting. Therefore, the common private and public spaces must be perfectly defined. A terrace can be suited for both, but if you want to use it for a particular purpose building high rise walls or changing the levels by adding stairs can be of great help to ensure privacy.

SIENDO UNA CASA DE PLAYA un lugar principalmente social y de descanso, se deben diferenciar perfectamente los espacios comunes privados de los públicos. Una terraza puede actuar con ambas cualidades pero si lo que se desea es definir su uso en función de una de ellas, la construcción de muros de gran altura o el cambio de niveles enfatizado por escaleras puede ser de gran ayuda para contener la privacidad.

PUISQU'UNE MAISON DE PLAGE est avant tout un endroit social et de repos, on doit marquer clairement la différence entre les espaces communs et ceux qui sont privés. Une terrasse peut avoir les deux qualités, mais si on désire définir son usage en fonction d'une d'entre-elles, les murs de grande hauteur ou le changement de niveaux souligné par des escaliers peut aider énormément à contenir ce qui est privé.

DADURCH, DASS EIN HAUS AM STRAND grundsätzlich ein sozialer Ort und ein Ort der Erholung ist, müssen die privaten Bereiche perfekt von den öffentlichen getrennt sein. Eine Terrasse kann beide Qualitäten haben, aber wenn man sie als eine dieser Funktionen definieren möchte, können hohe Mauern oder unterschiedliche Ebenen durch Treppen betont, dabei helfen die Privatsphäre zu waren.

AS FAMILY LIFE is one of the most important aspects of our daily lives, a dining room turns out to be an excellent choice to add life to our terrace and lead to different interactions between people. It is important to distinguish the covered areas from those that may be completely outdoors, and this can be done by adding colored cushions or a floral arrangement on the center of the table.

SI LA VIDA FAMILIAR es uno de las acciones más importantes de nuestra cotidianidad, un comedor resulta ser una excelente opción para darle vida a nuestra terraza y propiciar diversas interacciones entre las personas. Es importante distinguir las zonas a cubierto de aquellas que puedan estar totalmente a la intemperie, esto se puede lograr introduciendo cojines de colores o un arreglo floral al centro de la mesa.

SI LA VIE EN FAMILLE est une des actions les plus importantes de notre quotidien, une salle à manger est une excellente option pour animer notre terrasse et favoriser les interactions entre les personnes. Il est important de distinguer les zones couvertes de celles qui peuvent demeurer totalement sans abri ; on peut y réussir en ajoutant des coussins en couleurs ou un bouquet au centre de la table.

DAS FAMILIENLEBEN ist eine der wichtigsten alltäglichen Aktionen, ein Esstisch kann eine hervorragende Möglichkeit sein, unserer Terrasse Leben zu verleihen und verschiedenste Interaktionen zwischen den Personen zu ermöglichen. Es ist wichtig, die überdachten Zonen von denen, die vollständig im Freien sind, zu unterscheiden, was man durch farbige Kissen oder einem Blumenarrangement auf dem Tisch erreichen kann.

THE INDOOR AREA CAN BE DISTINGUISHED PERFECTLY from the outside area through the use of different light temperatures, as well as the use textures and finishing touches in the furniture. To create an ideal resting area, it is important to monitor the layout of all the elements to highlight the functional qualities and spatial virtues of the architectural design, as well as their relationship with the natural environment.

EL AMBIENTE INTERIOR PUEDE DISTINGUIRSE PERFECTAMENTE del exterior a través de la temperatura de la luz, así como de las texturas y los acabados del mobiliario empleado. Para que el descanso sea verdaderamente satisfactorio es importante vigilar la disposición de todos los elementos para resaltar las cualidades funcionales y virtudes espaciales del diseño arquitectónico así como su relación con el entorno natural.

ON PEUT PARFAITEMENT DISTINGUER L'AMBIANCE INTÉRIEURE de l'extérieur au moyen de la température de la lumière, ainsi que des textures et des finitions du mobilier. Pour que le repos soit vraiment satisfaisant, il est important de veiller à la disposition de tous les éléments pour souligner les qualités fonctionnelles et les vertus spatiales du design de l'architecture, ainsi que sa relation avec l'entourage naturel.

DAS AMBIENTE IM INNENBEREICH kann perfekt durch die Temperatur des Lichts, sowie die Texturen und die Verarbeitung der Möbel, vom Aussenbereich unterschieden werden. Damit das Ausruhen wirklich befriedigend ist, ist es wichtig die Verfügbarkeit aller Elemente zu prüfen, um die funktionellen Qualitäten und die räumliche Kraft des architektonischen Designs sowie seine Beziehung zu der natürlichen Umgebung, zu betonen.

DOUBLE-HEIGHT SPACES allow for cross-ventilation, which keeps temperatures much more stable and pleasant during the day. By covering the walls with volcanic stone you will add a rustic personality to the area, which combines really well with large cotton curtains. And the correspondence of colors and textures between chairs, cushions or mats will add a sophisticated look to the space.

LOS ESPACIOS CON DOBLE ALTURA permiten obtener una ventilación cruzada que propicia que el confort térmico al emplearlos durante el día sea mucho mayor. Recubrir los muros con piedra volcánica le dará una personalidad rústica que sin dejar de ser encantadora se conjugará muy bien con grandes cortinas de algodón. La correspondencia de colores y texturas entre sillas, cojines o tapetes favorecerá de manera sofisticada la apariencia del espacio.

LES ESPACES À DOUBLE HAUTEUR peuvent permettre d'obtenir une ventilation croisée qui favorise le confort thermal pendant la journée. Revêtir les murs de pierre volcanique ajoutera à la personnalité rustique qui, tout en étant toujours charmante, se conjuguera fort bien avec de grands rideaux de coton. La correspondance de couleurs et textures entre les chaises, les coussins et les tapis favorisera d'une manière sophistiquée l'apparence de l'espace.

BEREICHE IN DOPPELTER HÖHE erlauben eine bessere Belüftung, die am Tage den Komfort erheblich steigert. Die mit Vulkangestein verkleideten Mauern haben eine rustikale Persönlichkeit, die ohne den Charme zu verlieren, sehr gut zu den grossen Vorhängen aus Baumwolle passt. Die passenden Farben und Texturen der Stühle, Kissen oder Teppiche, kommen dem Aussehen des Bereiches in raffinierter Weise zugute.

The functionality and versatility of this area is centered on the possibility of using different corners that act as places to sit in as a group, as a couple, or just alone, while enjoying a good read during dusk.

La funcionalidad así como la versatilidad de este espacio se fundamenta en la posibilidad de utilizar diversos rincones que actúan como lugares para sentarse en grupo, en pareja o, simplemente a solas, para gozar de una buena lectura al atardecer.

La fonctionnalité ainsi que la versatilité de cet espace est fondée sur la possibilité d'utiliser divers coins qui deviennent des endroits pour s'assoir en groupe, en couple, ou simplement tout seul, afin de jouir d'une bonne lecture à la tombée du soir.

Die Funktionalität und die Vielseitigkeit dieses Bereiches basiert auf der Möglichkeit verschiedene Ecken zu nutzen, die als Plätze agieren, um sich mit einer Gruppe zu setzen, zu zweit oder einfach allein, um eine gute Lektüre beim Sonnenuntergang zu geniessen.

WHEN THE NATURAL LOCATION of the site allow us to have a privileged field of vision, you should consider including oversized furniture that will allow us to spend long hours of relaxation. A small pergola or wood deck will generate a microclimate that is appropriate to cope with thermal variations from other areas. Color can be present in ornaments and furniture of greater visual presence.

CUANDO LOS RELIEVES NATURALES del sitio nos permiten tener un campo visual privilegiado debe considerarse incluir muebles de gran tamaño que nos permitan pasar largas horas de relajación. Una pequeña pérgola o cubierta de madera generará un microclima bastante oportuno para sobrellevar las variaciones térmicas propias de un espacio exterior. El color puede tener presencia en los elementos de mayor jerarquía sensorial.

QUAND LES RELIEFS NATURELS de l'endroit nous permettent d'avoir un champ visuel privilégié on doit penser à inclure des meubles de grande taille qui nous permettent de passer de longues heures de détente. Une petite pergola ou une toiture en bois génère un microclimat assez utile pour supporter les variations thermales d'un espace extérieur. La couleur peut faire sentir sa présence dans les éléments de plus haute hiérarchie sensorielle.

WENN DAS NATÜRLICHE RELIEF der Umgebung uns erlauben einen ausserordentlichen Ausblick zu haben, sollte man in Betracht ziehen grosse Möbel zu verwenden, die uns erlauben lange Stunden der Entspannung zu verbringen. Eine kleine Pergola oder ein Holzdach schafft ein günstiges Mikroklima um den unterschiedlichen Wetterbedingungen denen man draussen ausgesetzt ist, zu trotzen. Die Elemente die als am Wichtigsten empfunden werden, können mit Farben betont werden.

# architecture arquitectónicos architectoniques architekten

3 *architectural project:* ABAX, fernando de haro l., jesús fernández s., omar fuentes e., bertha figueroa p.

4-5 *architectural project:* H PONCE ARQUITECTOS, henry ponce

8 *architectural project:* ELÍAS RIZO ARQUITECTOS, elías rizo s., alejandro rizo s.

9 *architectural project:* GRUPO ARQUITECTÓNICA, genaro nieto ituarte

10 (left) *architectural project:* ARQUIPLAN, bernardo hinojosa

11 (left) *architectural project:* ART ARQUITECTOS, antonio rueda

11 (right) *architectural project:* QUINTANILLA ARQUITECTOS, alejandro quintanilla o., alejandro quintanilla m.

14-17 *architectural project:* ABAX, fernando de haro l., jesús fernández s., omar fuentes e., bertha figueroa p.

20-21 *architectural project:* GRUPO ARQUITECTÓNICA, genaro nieto ituarte

22-23 *architectural project:* ERNESTO VELA RUIZ (E) STUDIO, ernesto vela ruiz, oswaldo muñoz m.

26-27 *architectural project:* a.a.a. ALMAZÁN ARQUITECTOS Y ASOCIADOS, guillermo almazán c., guillermo suárez a., dirk thurmer f.

30 *architectural project:* ABAX, fernando de haro l., jesús fernández s., omar fuentes e., bertha figueroa p.

32-33 *architectural project:* MUÑOZ ARQUITECTOS ASOCIADOS, javier muñoz m.

36-37 *architectural project:* GRUPO ARQUITECTÓNICA, genaro nieto ituarte

38-39 *architectural project:* ABAX, fernando de haro l., jesús fernández s., omar fuentes e., bertha figueroa p.

42-43 *architectural project:* ABAX, fernando de haro l., jesús fernández s., omar fuentes e., bertha figueroa p.

46-47 *architectural project:* ABAX, fernando de haro l., jesús fernández s., omar fuentes e., bertha figueroa p.

48-49 *architectural project:* GRUPO ARQUITECTÓNICA, genaro nieto ituarte

50-51 *architectural project:* ELÍAS RIZO ARQUITECTOS, elías rizo s., alejandro rizo s.

53 *architectural project:* ABAX, fernando de haro l., jesús fernández s., omar fuentes e., bertha figueroa p.

54-55 *interior design project:* COVILHA, blanca gonzález, maribel gonzález, mely gonzález

56-57 *architectural project:* MURO ROJO ARQUITECTURA, elizabeth gómez c., jorge medina

58-59 *architectural project:* SERRANO MONJARAZ ARQUITECTOS, juan pablo serrano o., rafael monjaraz f. / R.ZERO, edgar velasco c.
*interior design project:* isabel maldonado

60-61 *architectural project:* ABAX, fernando de haro l., jesús fernández s., omar fuentes e., bertha figueroa p.

62-63 *interior design project:* COVILHA, blanca gonzález, maribel gonzález, mely gonzález

64-65 *architectural project:* GRUPO ARQUITECTÓNICA, genaro nieto ituarte

68-69 *architectural project:* CORNISH ARQUITECTOS, jorge cornish a.

71 *architectural project:* ABAX, fernando de haro l., jesús fernández s·, omar fuentes e., bertha figueroa p.

73 (bottom) *architectural project:* ABAX, fernando de haro l., jesús fernández s·, omar fuentes e., bertha figueroa p.

74-75 *architectural project:* LASSALA + ELENES ARQUITECTOS, carlos lassala m., eduardo lassala m., diego mora d., guillermo r. orozco

76-77 *architectural project:* FÉLIX BLANCO DISEÑO Y ARQUITECTURA, félix blanco m.

78-79 *interior design project:* COVILHA, blanca gonzález, maribel gonzález, mely gonzález

82-83 *architectural project:* BROISSIN ARCHITECTS, gerardo broissin, rodrigo jiménez, mauricio cristóbal

84 *architectural project:* CGS ARQUITECTOS, arturo chico c., rodrigo gonzález s., pedro shveid s.

86-87 *architectural project:* ANONIMOUS-LED, alfonso jiménez e., marco a. velázquez a., jorge plascencia a., vittorio bonetti

89 *architectural project:* CIBRIAN ARQUITECTOS, fernando cibrian

91 *architectural project:* CIBRIAN ARQUITECTOS, fernando cibrian

92-93 *architectural project:* ELÍAS RIZO ARQUITECTOS, elías rizo s., alejandro rizo s.

94-95 *architectural project:* DE REGIL ARQUITECTOS, luis alonso de regil g. m.

96-97 *architectural project:* ABAX, fernando de haro l., jesús fernández s., omar fuentes e., bertha figueroa p.

99 *architectural project:* ABAX, fernando de haro l., jesús fernández s., omar fuentes e., bertha figueroa p.

100-101 *architectural project:* DE REGIL ARQUITECTOS, luis alonso de regil g. m.

102-103 *architectural project:* REIMS ARQUITECTURA, eduardo reims h., jorge reims h.

104 *architectural project:* ABAX, fernando de haro l., jesús fernández s., omar fuentes e., bertha figueroa p.

105 *architectural project:* JUAN IGNACIO CASTIELLO ARQUITECTOS, juan ignacio castiello c.

106 *architectural project:* CENTRAL DE ARQUITECTURA, josé sánchez, moisés isón

108 *architectural project:* ERNESTO VELA RUIZ (E) STUDIO, ernesto vela ruiz, oswaldo muñoz m.

110-111 *architectural project:* ARMELLA ARQUITECTOS, mario armella g.

112-113 *architectural project:* ABAX, fernando de haro l., jesús fernández s., omar fuentes e., bertha figueroa p.

114-115 *architectural project:* ARCO ARQUITECTURA CONTEMPORÁNEA, josé lew kirsch, bernardo lew kirsch

116-117 *architectural project:* TAAG ARQUITECTURA, gerardo ayala g.

118-119 *architectural project:* H PONCE ARQUITECTOS, henry ponce

121 *architectural project:* GLR ARQUITECTOS, gilberto l.rodríguez

122-123 *architectural project:* RDLP ARQUITECTOS, rodrigo de la peña l.

125 *architectural project:* ULISES CASTAÑEDA SALAS ARQUITECTOS, ulises castañeda s.

126-127 *architectural project:* JUAN IGNACIO CASTIELLO ARQUITECTOS, juan ignacio castiello c.

128-129 *architectural project:* CENTRAL DE ARQUITECTURA, josé sánchez, moisés isón

131 *architectural project:* ARQUIPLAN, bernardo hinojosa

133 *architectural project:* H PONCE ARQUITECTOS, henry ponce

134-135 *architectural project:* MAYER HASBANI, mayer hasbani

136-137 *architectural project:* ARQUIPLAN, bernardo hinojosa

138 *architectural project:* JUAN CARLOS AVILÉS IGUINIZ, juan carlos avilés i.

140-141 *architectural project:* REIMS ARQUITECTURA, eduardo reims h., jorge reims h.

142-143 *architectural project:* GRUPO ARQUITECTÓNICA, genaro nieto ituarte

144 *architectural project:* CENTRAL DE ARQUITECTURA, josé sánchez, moisés isón

146-147 *architectural project:* ERNESTO VELA RUIZ (E) STUDIO, ernesto vela ruiz, oswaldo muñoz m.

149 *architectural project:* URIBE + ARQUITECTOS, oscar uribe v.

150 *architectural project:* MURO ROJO ARQUITECTURA, elizabeth gómez c., jorge medina

151 *architectural project:* CENTRAL DE ARQUITECTURA, josé sánchez, moisés isón

152-153 *interior design project:* COVILHA, blanca gonzález, maribel gonzález, mely gonzález

155 *interior design project:* EXTRACTO, arte, arquitectura y diseño, vanessa patiño, robert duarte

156-157 *architectural project:* DE REGIL ARQUITECTOS, luis alonso de regil g. m.

159 *architectural project:* CENTRAL DE ARQUITECTURA, josé sánchez, moisés isón

160 (top) *architectural project:* JUAN CARLOS ZORRILLA PURÓN, juan carlos zorrilla p.

160 (bottom) *architectural project:* CENTRAL DE ARQUITECTURA, josé sánchez, moisés isón

162-163 *architectural project:* ABAX, fernando de haro l., jesús fernández s., omar fuentes e., bertha figueroa p.

165 *architectural project:* CENTRAL DE ARQUITECTURA, josé sánchez, moisés isón

166-167 *architectural project:* ABAX, fernando de haro l., jesús fernández s., omar fuentes e., bertha figueroa p.

168-169 *interior design project:* CDS C-CHIC design studio, olga mussali h., sara mizrahi e.

171 *architectural project:* MICHEAS ARQUITECTOS, antonio micheas v.

172-173 *interior design project:* ESTUDIO ADÁN CÁRABES, adán cárabes

174 *architectural project:* H PONCE ARQUITECTOS, henry ponce

176 *architectural project:* SAMA ARQUITECTOS, rafael sama r., héctor alfonso g.

178 *architectural project:* MURO ROJO ARQUITECTURA, elizabeth gómez c., jorge medina

179 *architectural project:* CENTRAL DE ARQUITECTURA, josé sánchez, moisés isón

180-181 *architectural project:* SERRANO MONJARAZ ARQUITECTOS, juan pablo serrano o. / *interior design project* SERRANO MONJARAZ ARQUITECTOS, juan pablo serrano o., rafael monjaraz f.

185 *architectural project:* PASCAL ARQUITECTOS, gerard pascal, carlos pascal

187 *interior design project:* ESTUDIO ADÁN CÁRABES, adán cárabes

188-189 *architectural project:* GRUPO ARQUITECTÓNICA, genaro nieto ituarte

190-191 *architectural project:* ELÍAS RIZO ARQUITECTOS, elías rizo s., alejandro rizo s.

193 *architectural project:* ELÍAS RIZO ARQUITECTOS, elías rizo s., alejandro rizo s.

195-197 *architectural project:* ELÍAS RIZO ARQUITECTOS, elías rizo s., alejandro rizo s.

198-199 *architectural project:* ABAX, fernando de haro l., jesús fernánde s., omar fuentes e., bertha figueroa p.

200-201 *architectural project:* QUINTANILLA ARQUITECTOS, alejandro quintanilla o., alejandro quintanilla m.

202 *architectural project:* BR ARQUITECTOS ASOCIADOS, jaime barba g., gerardo ramírez a.

204-205 *architectural project:* ELÍAS RIZO ARQUITECTOS, elías rizo s., alejandro rizo s.

206-207 *architectural project:* PGM ARQUITECTURA, patricio garcía m.

208-209 *architectural project:* ELÍAS RIZO ARQUITECTOS, elías rizo s., alejandro rizo s.

210-211 *architectural project:* GRUPO ARQUITECTÓNICA, genaro nieto ituarte

212 *architectural project:* ABAX, fernando de haro l., jesús fernández s., omar fuentes e., bertha figueroa p.

213 *architectural project:* A CREATIVE PROCESS, andrés saavedra

214-215 *architectural project:* QUINTANILLA ARQUITECTOS, alejandro quintanilla o., alejandro quintanilla m.

217 *architectural project:* QUINTANILLA ARQUITECTOS, alejandro quintanilla o., alejandro quintanilla m.

218-219 *architectural project:* GRUPO ARQUITECTÓNICA, genaro nieto ituarte

220-221 (left) *architectural project:* ZOZAYA ARQUITECTOS, enrique zozaya

221 (right) *architectural project:* PGM ARQUITECTURA, patricio garcía m.

222-227 *architectural project:* ABAX, fernando de haro l., jesús fernández s., omar fuentes e., bertha figueroa p.

228 *architectural project:* ELÍAS RIZO ARQUITECTOS, elías rizo s., alejandro rizo s.

230-231 *architectural project:* BR ARQUITECTOS ASOCIADOS, jaime barba g., gerardo ramírez a.

232-233 *architectural project:* PGM ARQUITECTURA, patricio garcía m.

234-235 *architectural project:* ELÍAS RIZO ARQUITECTOS, elías rizo s., alejandro rizo s.

236 *architectural project:* A CREATIVE PROCESS, andrés saavedra

238-239 *architectural project:* ABAX, fernando de haro l., jesús fernández s., omar fuentes e., bertha figueroa p.

241 *architectural project:* ZOZAYA ARQUITECTOS, enrique zozaya

242-243 *architectural project:* ABAX, fernando de haro l., jesús fernández s., omar fuentes e., bertha figueroa p.

244-245 *architectural project:* A CREATIVE PROCESS, andrés saavedra

246 *interior design project:* EXTRACTO, arte, arquitectura y diseño, vanessa patiño, robert duarte

248-249 *architectural project:* GRUPO ARQUITECTÓNICA, genaro nieto ituarte

250-251 *architectural project:* A CREATIVE PROCESS, andrés saavedra

252-253 *architectural project:* GRUPO ARQUITECTÓNICA, genaro nieto ituarte

255 *architectural project:* A CREATIVE PROCESS, andrés saavedra

256-257 *architectural project:* QUINTANILLA ARQUITECTOS, alejandro quintanilla o., alejandro quintanilla m.

# photography  fotográficos  photographiques  fotografen

alberto cáceres - pgs. 4-5, 118-119, 133, 174

alejandro rodríguez - pg. 121

alfonso de béjar - pgs. 68-69, 168-169, 172-173, 187

© beta-plus publishing - pgs. 10 (right), 18-19, 24-25, 29, 34-35, 40-41, 44-45, 66-67, 70, 72, 73 (top), 80-81, 182-183

francisco lubbert - pgs. 10 (left), 131, 136-137

gabriela ibarra - pgs. 76-77

guadalupe castillo - pgs. 76-77

héctor velasco facio - pgs. 9, 20-21, 36-37, 48-49, 54-55, 62 to 65, 78-79, 89, 91, 125, 138, 142-143, 152-153, 156-157, 160 (top), 188-189, 210-211, 218-219, 248-249, 252-253

jaime navarro - pgs. 56 to 59, 114, 150, 178, 185

jorge moreno - pgs. 26-27

jorge silva - pgs. 3, 14 to 17, 30, 38-39, 42-43, 46-47, 53, 71, 73 (bottom), 96-97, 116-117, 166-167, 198-199, 222 to 227

jorge taboada - pgs. 22-23, 108, 121 to 123, 146-147

leonardo palafox - pgs. 99, 112-113, 162-163, 166-167, 212-213, 236, 238-239, 242 to 245, 250-251, 255

leonardo walter - pgs. 155, 246

luis gordoa - pg. 151

marcos garcía - pgs. 8, 50-51, 74-75, 92-93, 190-191, 193, 195-197, 204-205, 208-209, 228, 234-235

mark callanan - pgs. 60-61, 104, 202

michael calderwood - pgs. 220-221(left), 241

mito covarrubias - pgs. 105, 126-127

pablo fernández del valle - pgs. 230-231

patricio garcía muriel - pgs. 206-207, 221 (right), 232-233

paul czitrom - pgs. 84, 106, 110-111, 128-129, 144, 159, 160 (bottom), 165, 179

paul rivera - pgs. 82-83

pedro hiriart - pgs. 94-95, 100-101, 156-157

peter myska - pgs. 11 (right), 200-201, 214-215, 217, 256-257

rafael gamo - pg. 176

raúl ramón - pg. 105

ricardo janet - pgs. 86-87, 102-103, 140-141

rolando córdoba - pgs. 32-33

sandra pereznieto - 180-181

sófocles hernández - pg. 11 (left)

víctor benítez - pgs. 134-135, 171

yoshihiro koitani - pg. 149

Editado en Junio 2012. Impreso en China. El cuidado de
esta edición estuvo a cargo de AM Editores, S.A. de C.V.
Edited in July 2012. Printed in China. Published by
AM Editores, S.A. de C.V.